Gambling with Philosophy

Where Chance Meets Decision Making

Stan Baronett

ALINEA

ALINEA

Alinea Learning

Boston, Massachusetts

Published in the United States by Alinea Learning, an imprint and division of Alinea Knowledge, LLC, Boston.

Visit our website at www.alinealearning.com.

Library of Congress Cataloging-in-Publication Data is available on file.

Print book ISBN: 979-8-9878531-8-4

eBook ISBN: 979-8-9878531-7-7

Cover photo and design copyright © 2023 by Carly Baronett

Contents

Preface

Gambling with Philosophy explores how chance is intimately involved in every part of our lives. It does this by developing a story where a decision to pursue a career in philosophy, and an interest in gambling, both come about through chance occurrences. The emphasis on chance as a natural random part of the world is contrasted with the common reference to "luck" as a metaphysical force that for some unknown mystical reason rewards the "lucky" few and hurts the "unlucky" majority of humans.

The relationship between chance and gambling is explored through a series of conversations between two people who meet on a train. They discuss the uncertainties inherent in sports betting, horse racing, and casino games. But the conversations also reveal the uncertainties—and gambles—inherent in all of life's decisions. The reasons for the main character's decisions involve the entanglement of early life experiences, education, and gambling.

The story proceeds through a series of conversations in which the characters discuss the works of real philosophers, scientists, and novelists. The discussions also include references to movies, music, and books that are also real; nevertheless, the quotes and references are used as part of a fictional dialogue in a fictional setting. For readers who might be interested, the sources of the quotes and references and where they can be found in the real world are noted at the back of the book.

The conversations illustrate how games of chance, cognitive biases, decision making, and the chance occurrences that occur throughout our lives present us with "gambles" involving uncertainties, the outcomes of which determine the course of our lives.

Chapter 1

TELLS

Excuse me, do you know if the train will be making a stop anytime soon?

As a matter of fact, the conductor is just getting ready to make a stop announcement.

"May I have your attention, please. We will arrive in Somerset station shortly. We will arrive in Somerset station— shortly."

You were right about the announcement. I imagine you must have travelled on this train before, so you know the stops.

I have travelled this route a few times, but that is not how I knew a stop was coming up.

Since there are many stops along the way, you guessed that one was due.

No, that is not how I knew. I have been observing the conductor for a while. Just before we reached each stop he raised his cap with his left hand and combed

8

his hair using the fingers of his right hand; then he took a deep breath, exhaled, slowly lifted himself up and walked to the microphone.

So you saw a pattern in his behavior.

Everyone forms patterns of behavior, especially when we perform repetitive tasks.

Don't they have a name?

You mean the patterns?

Yes.

I am sure that psychologists have a name for it, but the term I learned is "tell."

Isn't that the word that gamblers use? I think I remember hearing it when I watched a few poker tournaments on television.

Yes, it is a term used by poker players when they refer to facial expressions, movements, or speech patterns that telegraph what kind of hand a person has. For instance, in the movie *Rounders*, the main character, played by Matt Damon, suddenly realizes that his opponent's tell involves how he handles an Oreo cookie. Most tells are more subtle than the one depicted in that movie, so it takes a lot of exposure with a particular player to pick up on them. The best players train themselves to try to be tell-free.

Is that possible?

It is probably not possible to eliminate all tells, but most poker pros work closely with observers who study every move, so they are in position to notice anything that might be a tell. If you watch some of the poker shows you can see how each player tries to suppress his or her tells. For example, some players try to regulate their breathing and blinking. Some train themselves to count to a certain number, say ten, before each move they make no matter what the situation, such as before a bet, a call, a raise, or a fold. A quite common strategy after making a bet is to simply stare at the chips or at the middle of the table and not make eye contact with opponents. And many players now wear dark glasses, so their eyes are not visible.

Ah, the windows of the soul.

For poker pros, the eyes are the window to your hand, the poker hand you are betting. There has been a lot written about the eyes and how they relate to whether a player is bluffing or has a strong hand. Professional poker players read all the books, so this helps explain the wide-spread use of dark glasses. Some players have even resorted to wearing hoodies which they place over their head and close tightly so their opponent cannot see their face at all. But some still abide by the old school method of simply learning to have a good poker face.

So the best poker players don't have any tells?

I believe that everyone has tells, but the best players make them hard to discover. Nevertheless, information about players is available all the time they are sitting at a table, whether they are actively engaged in a hand or not. I think that if we could capture every body movement, facial expression, and speech pattern of a player over the course of hundreds of hours of playing time, and if that information could be transferred to a computer that had the right software to analyze the movements, the bets, and the outcomes of the hands, then the computer probably could find a tell in any player.

So anyone with access to that knowledge would always win.

It is not that simple. Remember that the best players train themselves to avoid having tells. Given this, any remaining subtle tells uncovered by the computer might be of minimal importance in an actual game. It might give you a slight edge, but it might not occur often enough, or in the right circumstances to guarantee that you will win. And of course, armed with your knowledge, you too would most likely develop tells that a pro is likely to recognize. So even though you might infer with a high probability that your opponent is bluffing, your opponent might just

11

as easily have access to your tells that might expose the trap you are setting.

It sounds like you studied this a lot.

Not as a scientist would. My experience is limited to a few circumstances early in my life.

Can you reveal any of it?

Oh sure, it is nothing that others do not already know, so I am not letting you in on any trade secrets. But it did provide me the opportunity and the financial backing to pursue what turned out to be my career— although I use that term loosely.

And what was that career, if I'm not being too presumptuous?

Not at all. I was a philosophy instructor.

Where did you teach?

Many places. I like to travel.

Did you have a position at a university that allowed you to travel but still come back to your school? What is that called—tenure?

Yes, "tenure" is the correct term.

And I believe that tenure requires you to publish or perish, is that right?

Not always. If you wish to have a permanent position, then many schools require you to pass through the tenure procedure. There are several requirements, one of which is publishing a certain number of articles in peer-reviewed journals, depending on the discipline. But many four-year colleges and community colleges do not require publications for advancement to tenure; those schools emphasize teaching. I was able to avoid the publish or perish requirement partly because I am restless and enjoy moving around.

Oh, we seem to have veered off track.

Is that a train joke?

No, no, I'm sorry, I didn't intend it to be funny.

No need to apologize. I thought it was a nice touch.

I meant that we got away from the point where you were going to explain to me how you got interested in tells and some of the experiences you had early in your life.

The first experience that I can connect to a payoff happened quite unexpectedly. I was with several of my friends in a bar where we were watching the local

National Football League team play one of its rivals. I was not a big fan of watching sports; I preferred to play. Anyway, at some point in the game I thought I noticed something odd. At first I thought that I was mistaken, but the more I watched I realized that I discovered a tell in the local team's quarterback. Of course, I did not call it a "tell" back then since I was not yet familiar with the term. It was amazingly simple. I saw two things. First, when the quarterback was under center waiting for the snap, and his feet were lined up directly across from each other, then it was a run play. But when he placed his right foot ever so slightly behind his left foot, then it was a pass play. I am sure that I had watched that quarterback play before, but before that night I never noticed his tell. After I watched him a few more times and when I knew I was right, I started making small bets with my friends about what the next play would be when we had the ball. I said that right before the snap I would predict whether it would be a run or pass. I won the bets, but I was not interested in trying to take money from my friends. It was just fun being able to see something that they could not see. We soon stopped betting after it became apparent that I was always right, but they still wanted me to make the predictions.

Did you reveal your secret to your friends? And did you use your knowledge to make bets with other people in other games?

No, I decided to keep it to myself, and I never used it after that to make bets. But after the game, I was approached by a man who said he was a scout for the local Major League Baseball team. He had been watching our group and noticed that my predictions were always correct, so he asked if I was just lucky. I said that I had noticed something in the quarterback that tipped me off to what play was coming up. He remarked that this could be important, and asked if I would be interested in talking to someone in the football team's organization. He said that if I were on to something, then maybe other teams had picked up on this and were using the knowledge on defense against the local team. He said that it could be quite beneficial to me. If I were interested, then he would take me to see one of the coaches. I had nothing to lose, so I gave him my phone number.

What kind of work were you doing at the time?

I was working full-time at the U.S. Post Office while I was also attending a university full-time.

How did you manage that?

By doing both badly.

No, seriously.

I am serious. I really could not successfully handle full-time undergraduate studies during the day, and a

15

full-time job at night. But I needed the money, and although I was not doing well in school, I was attracted to what was happening there. I thought everyone was intelligent, and I was fascinated by the discussions that went on in classrooms, although I did not follow much. It was like watching professional athletes perform, but with words and ideas. I had only experienced that thrill once in high school when my geometry teacher tried teaching us about truth tables, a part of logic. He took some sentences and explained how they could be mapped onto a table that listed all the true and false possibilities, and how certain combinations determined when those sentences were true and when they were false. It seemed so precise, simple, and clear. I did not know where it led or what it had to do with my everyday life, but it struck me as important in some way I could not articulate. It was my first real personal experience with high-level abstract thinking.

Much later, I came across Helen Keller's account of when she learned about words. An illness at a young age left her unable to see or hear, so she grew up without learning any language. But her teacher, Anne Sullivan, worked tirelessly trying to get Helen to connect the patterns of sign language movements that Anne pressed into Helen's palms. One day, Helen made a startling connection: "I stood still, my whole attention fixed upon the motions of her fingers. Suddenly I felt a misty consciousness as of something forgotten—a thrill of returning thought; and somehow the mystery of language was revealed to me. I knew then that w-a-t-e-r meant the wonderful cool something that was flowing over my hand. The living word awakened my soul, gave it light, hope, set it free!" Helen was instantly transported into the world of ideas.

I can't imagine what her transition must have felt like. Most of us can't remember learning language because it usually happens naturally and so slowly that we never realize that we are being introduced to the world of ideas.

Yes, and we usually cannot remember when we were confronted with abstractions which we come to accept. For instance, we start out thinking the world is flat, and then one day we are shown the Earth as a sphere. This must strike every child as an absurdity because it means that unless we are on top of the sphere we will fall off, the same way that anything that we place on a ball or a balloon would fall off. Our teachers realize this, so they then tell us that we are stuck to the Earth by a thing called "gravity," which, when I was in school, was shown as a large magnet inside Earth. The teachers must have assumed that every child would slap themselves in the forehead and say, "Of course, how could I be so stupid—gravity!" And as if that was not enough, we were also told that the Earth is spinning on its axis at around 1000 miles an hour, and the Earth is revolving around the Sun at about 60,000 miles an hour.

And yet somehow we come to accept it.

Everyone except the Flat-Earthers, a strange society of non-believers; they publish their own monthly magazine. Of course, there are many such leaps into abstraction that we go through without being conscious of when we finally accept them. For instance, why is the game of peek-a-boo so much fun for young children? You hide behind something and then jump out and the child is ecstatic. The giggling and sheer joy continues for as many times as you feel inclined to play the game. It provides an inexhaustible supply of fun, at least for the kid.

> *Yes, I often wondered why it seemed like so much fun. You would think the child would get bored with the game.*

Most likely it is because they have not yet reached the stage of awareness about the persistence of objects.

> *What do you mean?*

As an adult, you take it for granted that when an object goes behind something, the object still exists, even though you can no longer see it. Up until a certain age, children do not know this. That is why a young child cries when a parent leaves the house, because to the child the parent no longer exists, and the child does not know how to get the parent back.

Once the child transitions into the intellectual stage of "object permanence" the trauma begins to fade.

That makes sense.

And of course the child has no conscious awareness of this occurring, just like we do not recall when we fully accepted that we in fact live on a sphere and are currently spinning at 1000 miles an hour. Similarly, children eventually pass into the stage called "conservation." Before they reach that stage, they fail to understand that, for example, an amount of water stays the same no matter the shape of the container. There is a simple experiment anyone can do. Take a tall narrow glass, show it to a young child, and fill it to the top with water. Then show the child a long shallow pan. Have the child pour the water from the glass into the pan, and then fill the glass once again. Now ask the child if the pan or the glass contains more water. Until a child reaches the conservation stage, she will invariably say that the glass contains more water than the pan, even though she just poured the same full glass of water into the pan. And when the child eventually reaches the conservation stage, where she knows that both amounts of water are the same, she cannot recall ever having not known that fact.

I quickly recognized that people at the university were seeing and understanding the world radically different from me. They seemed to be in tune with abstractions and ideas that were many intellectual stages removed from where I was. And I longed to get to where they were.

And do you still feel that way?

Oh, yes. For example, I see the leading people in quantum physics, string theory, and black holes as people who passed into a stage of understanding that I will never attain. And there are entire fields of mathematics that are beyond my capacity to grasp. But unlike the child's passing naturally into the conservation stage, most highly abstract fields such as physics and mathematics are not stages that most of us can easily grow into. They might require a certain set of innate skills that not everyone has, but of course, this is pure speculation on my part.

If you don't mind my asking, how did you do in high school?

I did well, but simply because my school neither required nor expected much of us.

What do you mean?

Several years before I attended high school, the city school district had lots of discipline problems in the ten public high schools, so they devised a plan to consolidate the problem. My high school, which was centrally located, became known as "the dumping ground" for every problem student throughout the city. Those students would have to go to my high school until they were old enough to legally drop out. This resulted in my school slowly lowering the academic standards needed to graduate. Teachers were told to pass as many students as possible and not hold them back. This led to my school perennially being on the bottom of all city public high schools in academic performance.

Of course, when I arrived in ninth grade I had no way to judge the academic level of the school; I had nothing to compare it with. We rarely had homework, and we never finished a textbook for the entire school year. I did not mind. I liked that I did not have to spend time on homework or studying for tests because the tests were incredibly easy. I spent all my time after school playing sports with my neighborhood friends who also went to the same school.

When you became a senior did you plan to go to college?

No, I did not. I expected to follow my dad and work in a steel mill because the steel industry offered the best opportunity for work. Everyone I knew had at least one relative who worked at a steel mill. The network of different mills spanned twenty miles in any direction from where I grew up. You either worked for a steel mill, entered the military, worked at the Post Office, became a bartender, or hung out on street corners.

How did you manage to go to a university?

Mere chance. During my senior year we were told to fill out an application for a local university that had recently gone from being a private school to becoming a branch of the state's higher education system. This meant that the state would subsidize the cost of tuition, making it affordable to most students. As part of its agreement to become a state university, it had to agree to give all the city public school students admission priority for the next few academic years. Given this mandate, the university became less strict on its admission standards for local public school students. The result was that I was offered admission, and since the tuition was so inexpensive, I decided to give it a try. But I asked if I could start in the winter term instead of the fall because I wanted to work just in case college was not for me.

I recall you said that you worked for the Post Office. So you didn't wind up in a steel mill?

Here is what happened. After graduation, I applied to some steel mills and the Post Office at around the same time. I was called for an interview at a steel mill. My father told me that they would probably offer me a laborer job in the blooming mill, the worst place to work because of the danger. This is where the hot steel was handled, and the combination of complex machinery, constant loud noise, and red-hot metal resulted in lots of accidents. Of course, that is the job I was offered. I remember the interviewer saying that the job required working with hot metal, deep oil pits, dirty conditions, noise, and extremely dangerous equipment. He smiled and said, "So, do you think you would like to do that kind of work?" I told him, "No. I would not like doing that." He was somewhat taken aback, and asked if I was turning down the job offer. When I said that I would take the job, he seemed puzzled. "But you told me that you wouldn't like doing that kind of work." I said that anyone who liked to do that kind of work needs to be examined, but that I would do it since I needed a job. He did not seem happy with my explanation, but he gave me the job anyway. My dad said that they were usually desperate to fill those positions, so it was hard not to get an offer.

So you did work for a steel mill after all.

Once again, chance entered the scene. Since I was told to report to work the next Monday, I went home and bought a pair of steel-toed boots, a necessity for steel mill workers. The next day I got a call from the Post Office with an offer to be a mail clerk at the same hourly rate as the steel mill job. My choice was between the horrific working conditions in the blooming mill where extreme bodily damage was highly probable, or sorting one-ounce letters with the only danger being a paper cut.

An easy choice by all measures. I see how you wound up at the Post Office.

And since I did not want to quit the job at the end of summer, especially since I might not like university life, I asked to be admitted for the winter term. I was granted that option. When the winter term arrived, I registered for my classes and went to the bookstore. I was shocked. One of the courses required five books, and two other courses required three books. This was unexpected. I had never finished one book in an entire school year, and here I was expected to read multiple books in one semester.

What did you do?

I bought the books. Luckily, back then books were cheap. This was long before the book buyback system was introduced. Students generally kept their books, resulting in most college graduates having a small but useful home library. It was also a tangible connection to your degree.

Speaking of books, once upon a time books were physical things with physical pages and binding and glue and substantial front and back covers; things that you held in your hands. They had scents that you came to recognize and even sought out, perhaps a fine musty smell that brought back memories of certain passages in the book, passages that you could find because you remembered whether it was on a left-hand page or a right-hand page, or whether it was in the beginning, middle or end of the book. None of this is experienced with an eBook.

Of course we already saw this happen with mail. At one time, mail was a physical thing, delivered right to your door, perhaps affixed with colorful and exotic stamps from faraway places. Letter-writers attached part of their character and personality to the scrawl that you read repeatedly, not knowing when or if you would ever get another one. Now we have electronic mail. No paper, no handwriting in pencil, ink, or crayon to linger over. Sorry for the digression.

Not at all. I agree with your assessment. So, how did your first semester go?

I was completely overwhelmed. Daily homework, weekly quizzes, difficult exams, long written assignments, and the stark realization that I had to study to keep up. I was not amused.

How were your grades?

I was put on academic probation the first semester. And the second, and third semester as well. My assigned academic advisor said that although I had not yet achieved an overall GPA of 2.0, the minimum requirement to stay enrolled, I had kept creeping closer each semester, so they kept me on. Looking back, I believe it was because the university did not want to get rid of local students too soon after the university's admission into the state system. But after my fourth semester I managed to finally nudge past the 2.0 threshold.

That must have felt good.

It did. And as I said earlier, I liked hearing smart people discuss things in class. And although I did not grasp much of what my instructors were saying, I experienced glimmers of understanding, or at least I thought so, but I had a hard time reconstructing the ideas outside of class, so the thoughts had a short half-life. But since I accepted that what they were saying was important, I wanted to keep having that wash over me. And then one day in an introduction to philosophy class I said something—I do not recall what—and to my surprise, the teacher said that my remark was "interesting and probably right." That experience was electric. It was the first time I thought that maybe I could fit into that world.

I don't know what to say. That's a lot to chew over. But perhaps we can return to your story about the quarterback.

Sorry. It is easy to get derailed.

Oh my, another train joke.

Chapter 2

ODDS

The result of my chance meeting with the baseball scout led to my being introduced to the offensive coordinator for the local football team. He was told that I could accurately predict whether an upcoming offensive play was a pass or a run. But I had not yet told anyone how I could do it. The coordinator was understandably skeptical, so he decided to test me. He used film of a closed practice session that I could not have possibly seen, and he asked me to make some predictions of offensive plays. I told him that I could do it only a second or two before the ball was snapped. He began showing me plays and I got eight in a row correct, which was unlikely.

Why was it unlikely?

Based on simple probability calculations, it had a small chance of occurring. Suppose there are just two options for each play: pass or run. Suppose further that each option has an equal chance of being realized. If so, then you have a 50/50 chance of correctly picking each play before it happens. Another way of saying the same thing is that you have a 1 out of 2 chance of guessing correctly on each play. Therefore, the chance of correctly picking a random selection of eight plays in a row is ½ x ½ x ½ x ½ x ½ x ½ x ½ x ½ which is 1/256.

So that would be the odds of correctly picking eight coin tosses in a row, is that right?

Yes, it is the same odds for any game or situation where only two options are available, provided it is a fair game and you have all the relevant information.

What do you mean by a "fair game" and "all the relevant information"?

A fair game is one where there is no cheating, and all the relevant information regarding the factors that might affect the calculation of odds is readily available. For example, suppose I told you that an opaque jar contains only green and blue marbles. Now I want you to guess what color marble I will pick out of the jar. What are the odds of, say, my picking a green marble?

Based on our discussion about two choices, it would be 50/50.

You are assuming two important premises that I did not specify in the above scenario.

What do you mean?

First, I did not say it was a fair game. It could be a scam where I palm a marble to make sure you guess incorrectly. Second, I did not tell you the proportion of green and blue marbles. For example, suppose there were 30 green marbles and only 10 blue ones.

I see. You originally said there were only green and blue marbles but you didn't specify how many of each. Now I see what you mean by having all the relevant information. With the new information, it turns out that there are 40 marbles of which 30 are green. So there is a 75% chance of getting green on any random pick.

Correct. And that is why you need to know whether the game you are playing is a fair game and if you have all the relevant information. We can expand this discussion by stipulating that a fair game of chance with true odds is one where the probability of winning and losing are equal, and in the long run the gambler will break even. We know that a fair coin toss has an equal probability of coming up heads or tails, so each has a probability of 1/2. If you bet $1 on each toss of the coin, you will win the same number of times that you will lose—in the long run. Since there are one out of two chances of winning, one out of two chances of losing, true odds for this game are one-to-one, written as 1:1. So for every dollar you bet, you will get back $1 plus the $1 you bet, for a total of $2. And of course, if you lose, then your $1 is taken away.

The same idea holds for the toss of a die. The probability of the number 3 coming up on one toss of a die is 1/6, and the probability that 3 will not come up is 5/6. Given this, to ensure true odds for gambling purposes, if you bet that 3 will come up, you need to get odds of 5:1 in order to break even in the long run. If you decide to bet that 3 will not come up, then you have to be willing to give 5:1 odds to break even in the long run.

Knowing how to calculate true odds allows the gambler to recognize if the game is worth playing. All gamblers know that casino games do not provide true odds, and they accept that casinos need to make a profit to continue to operate, which they could not do if the games offered true odds. The odds are skewed in favor of the casino to ensure a winning margin, but sometimes the odds are so outrageous that smart gamblers will avoid playing those games.

What are some of those games?

Roulette provides one example of how the odds impact the player. Most American roulette wheels have 38 numbers, of which 18 are red, 18 are black, and two are green, 0 and 00. The probability that a red number will come up on any given spin is 18/38, and the probability that red will not come up is 20/38, so the odds are slightly against your winning if you bet red. The same holds for black. The casino offers 1:1 odds for this bet; that means you receive one

30

dollar from the casino plus the dollar you bet on red. Since these are not true odds, you can see that the casino is guaranteed to win in the long run.

But people do sometimes win, don't they?

Yes, of course, but that is usually in the short run. If that person continues to bet, then eventually they will wind up losing because the odds are stacked against their being able to win for a long period. Billion dollar casinos are built by the odds being in favor of the casino.

Okay, I see that betting red or black has odds that are against the player. But what happens if I bet a single number, say my lucky number 24?

If you decide to place your bet on your lucky number, here is what will happen. The casino is willing to give you 35:1 odds for this bet. But remember there are 38 numbers, so once again the casino is not giving you true odds. The casino will win in the long run.

I see that now. Please, continue with your football story.

The coordinator stopped showing me the plays. He called the head coach and said to meet us in the viewing room. The head coach arrived and was told what I had done. They proceeded to show me play after play, and after I got thirteen in a row correct, they all stared at me as if I were an alien. The head coach then said something I never expected: "How much do you want for this." At first, I did not know what he meant. I guess I must have looked puzzled, so he said that they would pay me not to tell other teams my secret. It had never occurred to me that what I had discovered might be highly valuable.

So what did you do?

Since I had no idea what my "skill" was worth, I kept silent. This seemed to make them nervous, and I imagine that they thought that I was playing hard to get, but really I was just dumbfounded by the prospect in front of me. As a way to gauge my financial intent, and as a way to ease the tension, someone asked me what I did. I told them I was a student at the local university and that I also worked at the Post Office. They asked me how much I made. At the time, I think I made around $2.50 an hour or about $5,000 a year before taxes. The coach said that they would hire me at $8,000 a year. I could set my own work schedule, and I wouldn't have to work more than twenty hours a week during football season, and fewer hours during the offseason. I would not have a supervisor, and I was told to relate my findings only to the coach, so the information would be kept on a need-to-know basis. My job title would be "scout," which is a general term that fits lots of positions in large professional sports organizations. They would set up a small room at the stadium for me where they would have each game's film broken down, so I could watch an entire game in an hour or so.

I told them that since there is no way to predict how many tells existed in the local team or their opponents, they should not expect daily or even weekly discoveries on my part. Therefore, it might take a considerable amount of time to discover other tells. I guess they thought I was playing hardball and negotiating for more money, but I was just being honest. In fact, it had only just dawned on me that I might never be able to discover another tell again. After a quick huddle, they upped my salary to $10,000 with the added bonus that should I have to spend more than 20 hours a week studying film, then I would get ten dollars an hour extra for anything over 20 hours of work.

That was a lot, considering what you were earning at the Post Office.

Since I had to work 40 hours a week at a terribly boring job, it was a windfall for me. My only concern was how long I could last in the position. I mean, if, after I told them my secret, I could not find anything else useful, they might dump me in a month. I told them that their terms were acceptable, but, in a flash of unexpected foresight, I said that I needed a two-year guaranteed contract because I would have no other income after I quit the Post Office, and I wanted to finish my undergraduate degree. They quickly agreed. We broke for lunch while they had the office draw up a contract. They took me to an old seafood restaurant near the stadium, a place my dad used to take me when I was young. I remember they had fish sandwiches so big that I could never finish one. I was determined not to let this fish get the best of me, and I proudly ate the entire sandwich, the first of many to come, in fact.

What happened next?

I signed the contract and told them my secret. They were flabbergasted, and at first could not believe it because it seemed so simple. They went through game after game, and sure enough, the tell was there. It actually became somewhat funny as they yelled in unison, "PASS" or "RUN" just before each play. They slapped each other on the back as if they were witnessing the first Moon landing. One of them said that this information was worth a million bucks to the team, but the head coach quickly added that it was not meant literally. They must have thought that I would be offended by my small salary in the face of such valuable information. I just sat there and smiled at my great fortune of having recognized something that apparently no one else had seen. This was a feeling I had never before experienced, and I thought maybe that is how the people that I admired went through life. Even if I never had another insight like this one, I was happy that I experienced it at least once.

*What did they do with the information? And
did you come up with any more tells?*

It was easy for them to correct their quarterback's
problem; all they had to do was have him practice
having one stance for every play. It did not take long
for the quarterback to learn to suppress his tell. At
that time there was no way to know whether any
other teams had spotted the tell. The only way to
directly verify that possibility was if a player from
another team was traded to the local team and he told
them that his old team had noticed it. But as long as
I was there, that never happened. What kept me in
good graces is that the teams in the division that we
lost to earlier that season eventually lost to us in the
return games, so that stood in my favor. After all, if
those teams had picked up on the tell, then it was no
longer available after I exposed it.

*Your team beat them in the return matches,
so that should prove they were aware of the
tell.*

"Prove" is a strong word, at least when it is used in
math, geometry, and logic. In those disciplines, it
means an argument in which, assuming the premises
are true, it is impossible for the conclusion to be
false. In other words, the conclusion follows
necessarily from the premises. But this is a logical
certainty, not a physical certainty. So, in the physical
world where the team corrected the quarterback's
stance and eliminated the tell, the positive results

35

supported the hypothesis that other teams may have known about the tell, but it does not follow necessarily from the information available.

I think I understand, but can you elaborate on that a bit?

A teacher of mine explained this in a lecture. He said to imagine that one day your car does not start. Your sister suggests that you probably have a dead battery. This is a hypothesis, a conjecture or explanation, if you will, and it is either true or false. We mere mortals cannot simply look at a car battery and straight-away determine whether it has any power. Your sister volunteers to help you disconnect the battery and then to drive you in her car to a shop where they can test your battery before you go out and buy a new one. The mechanic connects your battery to his battery-tester machine and soon is able to tell you the machine indicates that your battery has no power. You now have evidence that supports, confirms or verifies your sister's hypothesis.

That's straightforward.

Yes, if the information is accurate, then it verifies the hypothesis. So far, so good. But being a skeptical person, suppose you ask the mechanic if it is possible that his battery-tester machine is defective? The mechanic has to admit that it is possible.

Let me see where this is going. Before we went to the shop, we didn't know whether the battery was dead. But the battery-tester machine verified that it was dead. The question now becomes whether we have any evidence that the battery-tester machine is functioning properly.

Right. Of course, the mechanic will most likely assert that his machine is working properly. But until we have direct evidence to support that claim, it is another hypothesis. My teacher said that here is where the "skeptical nightmare," as he put it, points to its desired effect. In order to verify, or possibly refute, the mechanic's hypothesis, we need to take the battery-tester machine to the factory where it was built and have it hooked up to their battery-tester-tester machine, a machine that tests battery-testers.

Oh, this is funny. Suppose the battery-tester-tester machine says that the battery-tester machine is working properly. That would be evidence to verify the mechanic's hypothesis that his machine is working properly. But now we can ask the battery-tester factory how they know their battery-tester-tester machine is working properly. This is like a Monty Python routine. But I see the point.

To continue the thought experiment, suppose that instead of taking the battery to a mechanic, you decided to just go out and buy a new one. And suppose that after you installed it, your car started. Would that scenario verify the original hypothesis that your battery was dead?

Sure, why wouldn't it?

This is where we can see what else is involved in verifying or refuting a hypothesis. We rely on objective evidence to either support a hypothesis or to reject it. This is why we say that the car starting after installing a new battery verifies the hypothesis that the original battery was dead. But this creates another problem. It possible that the terminal heads that were connected to the original battery were loose, but after the new battery was installed, the terminal heads now were clamped tight. After all, if the heads were loose, then the electrical current was not being sent from the battery to enable the car to start.

Yes, that's possible. And it would mean that the original battery might have been good after all. So, although replacing the battery results in the car starting, that fact doesn't rule out the possibility that the old battery might have had power.

It seems, then, that both verifying and refuting a hypothesis are not simple things. And the idea behind our simple thought experiment illustrates how difficult it can be when scientists try to test their hypotheses. Good experiments have to be devised, and good evidence needs to be uncovered. The more abstract our hypotheses are, the more difficult it is to determine the truth.

I think we wandered off track again, but I enjoyed the new scenery.

My thoughts do go in strange directions. Let me continue. If I recall, we were talking about my work as a scout. During my first two years with the organization, I concentrated on the team's offense since this is where the potential for other teams to anticipate what the offense is going to do is crucial. I started with the personnel whose primary responsibility was handling the football. This included the quarterback, wide receivers, tight ends, and running backs. Since I had spotted the quarterback's tell that I talked about earlier, I decided to concentrate on the foot placement of all the key personnel. This meant that I had to look at the same play many times, and since this was before computers and other devices made this type of analysis easy, the manual nature of rewinding the film over and over again made it time-consuming.

Why did you have to do repeated viewings of the same play?

On any given offensive play several things can happen, but we can narrow it down to either a pass play or a running play. If I were analyzing a pass play, then I needed to look at the quarterback, all the receivers, and the running backs, because they can either pass, run, or catch the ball. That meant looking at the foot placement of anywhere from four to six key players. What I needed to determine was if any of those players had a tell that indicated a pass or run play. But of course, a tell exists only if it is a repeated behavior. That entailed making notes for each player and annotating and updating those notes when I looked at subsequent plays and games.

That seems like a lot of tedious work.

It was, but I did not mind, especially because I was left alone. No one supervised me or looked over my shoulder, or even paid attention to how many hours I spent working, because I had access to the film room any time I wanted. Quite often, I was the only one there. I eventually expanded my research to include hand and arm placement. For example, a receiver might unconsciously place his hands on his hips as he lined up for a pass play, but then unconsciously place his arms straight down at his sides before a run play.

It's no wonder it took you so many hours to investigate whether tells exist. And since the offense has so many players involved, including back-up players who may not play every down, that adds up to a lot of work.

But all the work paid off when I was able to discover a new tell. The coaches loved it when they could explain it to a player and eliminate the tell. But it eventually occurred to me that correcting it immediately might not be the best strategy.

Why not?

If other teams already discovered a tell in one of our players, then they would be looking for it as a tipoff. So, instead of correcting a tell, I said that we should use it against the opposing team. For example, if our player had a tell that indicated a pass play, then we should have that player display the tell, but do it for a running play. That way the other team would be misled and would be expecting a pass play, so their defense would be out of position.

That's clever. You use the other team's recognition of a tell against them.

That is what good poker players do, too. They purposely set up a false tell early in the session, and then use it against their opponents later on when it benefits them most, say for a large pot.

Anyway, that is how my first two years went. I then branched out to the defensive players and looked for tells that might be tipping off the opposing team's offense to the type of defensive scheme that was deployed. Those tells allowed clever quarterbacks to change the play by calling an audible just before the ball was snapped; in other words, changing the play to take advantage of what the defense was planning to do.

How long did you stay at the job?

Five years.

Chapter 3

TRACKS

It took me three more years to finish my bachelor's degree, one more than I expected, and then I spent two additional years working as a scout. Although the pay was good, I was getting restless, a trait that determined most of my adult life. When I decided to quit, my family and friends thought I was crazy, especially since I had decided to try to be a full-time horse racing handicapper.

> *By "handicapper" I assume you mean a gambler, or as the British call it a "punter." I think the British use of the term stems from the idea of punting a rugby ball. When you punt you have some expectation of where the ball will go, but not with certainty. So a punter is anyone who takes a chance, including sports betting. But I'm not sure if that origin of the term is correct.*

I like it even if it is not correct, especially the idea of uncertainty. A handicapper is someone who spends a lot of time digesting information in order to make an "informed bet," meaning a bet that has some historical or statistical backing which is meant to reduce the uncertainty involved in any wager. Notice I say "reduce." The uncertainty never reaches zero because every horse race and sporting event has variables that cannot be controlled. My quitting a paying job for the unknown was definitely a gamble, but it was something that I wanted to do at the time.

So, you didn't think about going to graduate school?

Although I had thought about it, ultimately I determined that I was not quite ready, for a variety of reasons. My being on probation for the first two years at college meant that my final GPA was barely over 3.0, at the low end of the B range. I thought that my chances of being accepted into graduate school were quite low, so I put off the idea of applying. Years later, I decided to give it a try, and it turns out that the time off worked to my advantage. But that story can wait until after I relate the five years I spent handicapping races.

I decided to get away from the northeast's cold winters, so I went to south Florida. Besides the great weather, the area boasts year-round horse racing. I bought all the available horse racing books written by professional handicappers hoping to gain the knowledge they acquired over their lifetimes. Most of the books contained systems that revolved around data collection and analysis. Some systems were simple and others were complex, but in order to understand the basic principles behind the different systems, you need to know the kinds of factors that go into racing. Horse races are diverse, and that diversity makes it quite challenging. I will list some of the most important, and then go into details.

Since not all horses have equal physical abilities, there are different levels of competition. The highest level are Grade 1 races, also known as stakes races, such as the Kentucky Derby. These races offer the highest purses—the amount of money the winning owner receives. These races regularly have a purse of a million dollars, but recently a few countries began outdoing each other to attract attention, with one country offering twenty million for one race.

So the winning owner gets twenty million?

No, the money is usually spread out among all the runners. This varies from state to state and racing jurisdiction, but the average is around 60% of the purse to the winner, 20% to the second place horse, 10% for third, 5% for fourth, and each of the other runners split the remaining 5%. This is done to incentivize owners to enter their horses, even if they do not have a great chance of winning.

That makes sense, especially since I imagine that owning and training a racehorse is an expensive proposition.

Very expensive. The monthly training fee can run from $2000 a month to $5000, and that might not include veterinarian fees. Although many owners get into the business because of the chance to have a superstar horse, many day-to-day owners face a losing scenario. But yearly expenses can be deducted for tax purposes.

That would make it attractive to rich business people. They get tax deductions and the possibility of owning a famous racehorse.

Yes, a lot of it is driven by ego. I will skip some of the racing levels and mention just a few more. An important level is called "claiming races," which are the majority of races throughout the United States. In these races, the horses can be claimed—purchased—by other horse owners. The claiming price is set ahead of time, so everyone knows what they are getting into. As you can imagine, these are horses that the owners are willing to give up, if another owner is willing to pay the claiming price. The claiming costs can vary wildly, from as low as a few thousand dollars to $100,000 depending on the horse's perceived ability.

I can claim one of those horses?

No. Recall that I said that other horse owners can claim them. What you can do is purchase a horse privately from an owner, or buy one at an auction, and then register yourself as an owner at a racetrack. Then you can start claiming other horses.

I see. I can't just walk into a racetrack and start claiming horses. That makes sense.

I will do two more levels. Allowance races are for horses that are not quite in the stakes level, but are deemed better than claiming horses. Horses entered in allowance races cannot be claimed. The purses are higher than for claiming races but considerably smaller than stakes races. The last one I will talk about are maiden races, which are exclusively for horses that have not yet won a race. As soon as your horse wins a maiden race, it must move to other levels.

Can we go back a little bit? I recall you mentioned the Kentucky Derby. Can anyone enter a horse in that race?

That is a good question, and one that a lot of people ask. The three races that make up the Triple Crown are the ones most people know about: The Kentucky Derby, the Preakness, and the Belmont. But what a lot of people do not know is that those races are exclusively for three-year-old horses. That means that a horse gets only one shot to win it.

No wonder it has attained such a high status. A horse has one and only one chance of winning it. And that makes winning the Triple Crown even more special since all three have to be won in the same year.

It is extremely difficult. Only thirteen horses in around 150 years have done it as of 2022. So it is quite special. And that prestige is why owners are willing to spend millions to buy a young horse. Since there are around 20,000 thoroughbreds born each year, your chances of owning the winner are about one in twenty thousand.

That's long odds, but I can see why people would chase that dream.

We have covered one data point in handicapping: the race level. I will list a few more without going into too much detail, to illustrate why handicapping can be so time-consuming, and why picking winners means having to analyze and evaluate numerous variables.

Although there are around 75 thoroughbred race tracks in the United States, most of them have limited race meets. For example, the three major race tracks in New York—Saratoga, Aqueduct, and Belmont—split the year up so only one of them conducts racing at a time. Only a few tracks conduct year-long racing. Horses needing to ship between tracks means the horses are confronted with varying track types. Although most races in the U.S. are on dirt, there are often substantial differences between what the dirt contains. Some contain varying amounts of clay or sand, leading to substantial differences in how a horse moves over the surface. A given horse may prefer one racing surface over another, so how it performs may be radically different at each track.

You cannot assume that a horse who has run well at one track will run the same at another track, even if the tracks are in the same state.

When the weather is good, or in warmer states, a lot of races are on turf, the horse racing term for grass. Some horses do better on grass than dirt, and vice versa. A third kind of racing surface is called "synthetic," which is the common name for surfaces made from different blends of recycled carpet fibers, polypropylene, recycled rubber, and sand, with the mixtures usually coated in wax.

Why so many different surfaces?

Although many European and Asian race tracks conduct their races exclusively on turf, the United States tracks evolved mostly through the use of dirt. The differences in the composition of the dirt tracks is a result of most states using the soil at hand, along with percentages of clay and sand. Synthetic tracks were created as a way to reduce the effects of horse racing on horse's legs, since those surfaces are more forgiving than dirt. And racing on grass is not as punishing as dirt racing.

Do horses often switch racing surfaces?

Most trainers have an idea which surface should best fit their horse, but they will not know for sure until they train and run a few races over the surfaces. The different surfaces lead to handicapping problems, not only when horses change tracks but also when they change from dirt to turf, or to synthetic. That is why past data of a horse's performances at different tracks and on different surfaces is valuable information, and it is a major variable in trying to predict winners. Another important variable to consider when trying to pick winners is the weight that is assigned for each horse to carry.

What do you mean?

If a race requires each horse to carry the same weight, say 124 pounds, then since jockeys do not weigh the same, lead weights are added to the gear strapped around a horse, so the total weight of the jockey, the saddle, and the lead weights will have to be 124 pounds. If a jockey weighs more than 124, then no extra lead weight has to be added. Many races assign different weights depending on the relative abilities of each horse. This is done to, theoretically, give all the horses an equal chance to win.

Wait a minute. If my horse is better than your horse, then mine will be burdened with carrying more weight than yours?

It might, depending on the kind of race.

That doesn't seem fair.

I agree. Let me try to explain the race track's reasoning for this strange fact. Race tracks have to compete with each other for the limited amount of available horses at any one time. One way to do that is to protect owners from constantly having to run their horses against superior horses, with little chance that their horse will win. Making a superior horse carry more weight is meant to make a race more equitable. If an owner is at a track where her horses are being dominated by other horses, she will look for easier places to run.

> *It still seems weird to me. Why punish a horse for being able to run faster than other horses?*

I think that is one of the reasons why horse racing has a hard time attracting fans. I cannot think of another sport where the superior athletes are punished for being great athletes. Imagine a 100-yard footrace where the world's fastest runner has to start 10 yards behind everyone else, or has to carry extra weight strapped to his waist. Or suppose the heavyweight boxing champion has to fight with one hand tied behind his back. Or team sports where a basketball team has to compete with only four players against five.

> *That would be silly.*

Yes, and it is why some great horses were hindered in their careers because they were forced to compete under unequal conditions. The public likes to follow winners, especially ones that remain superior to all comers for a long time. But horse racing worries that a superior horse will scare away owners from competing if they cannot win a large stakes prize. To me, it does not matter how many owners choose to compete against the best horse. Let a superstar horse face as many or as few opponents as dare to challenge the champion, but do not try to make the champion lose. Why not showcase the best against all comers at equal weights? This is a big mistake that horse racing has made.

That is puzzling. If I owned a horse that couldn't quite match up with a superstar, then I might like the unequal assignment of weights. On the other hand, if I owned the superstar, then I would hate it.

We just need to look at a few more variables. Horses are often entered in races of varying length. A horse may race one time at a mile, and then in its next race run at six furlongs—a furlong is one-eighth of a mile, so six furlongs is three-fourths of a mile. Good data will tell you at which distance a given horse excels.

Another major variable is the track condition, usually designated as fast, good, sloppy, and muddy for dirt races; firm, good, yielding, soft, and heavy for turf races. Once again, it is important to know the kind of racing surface on which a horse does its best running.

I recall reading about some gambling groups, often called "syndicates," in Hong Kong that employed computer programmers to analyze one hundred variables for each horse race.

*I never realized that picking a winner
entailed evaluating and analyzing that
many possible variables. It seems quite
daunting to have to assess so many things
that can affect a horse race. So, how did
that group do?*

From what I read, certain groups won more than a
hundred million dollars, but since the people
involved do not want to reveal too much information,
the truth has not been independently verified. I
suspect that handicapping systems that can
accurately compile, analyze, and evaluate complex
variables can give you an edge in betting horse races.
But the edge you gain may be so small that it requires
betting large amounts to maximize your profits. As
an analogy, if I can get .05 percent interest on my
investment, it will make a tremendous difference
whether I can invest $100 or $10,000,000.

That makes perfect sense.

Most daily handicappers do not have extensive
computer programming skills, or large sums of
money to bet, so they rely a lot on "intuition," the
way a car mechanic does, using years of experience
to quickly assess the importance of certain pieces of
information. If you are familiar with the original Star
Trek TV series, Scotty, the ship's engineer would
often say that although the computers and

instruments do not indicate any problems, the ship just did not feel right to him.

I do remember him saying that, and I think all of us rely on something like that when we gain enough experience with something.

It is the feeling that you get when you combine extensive experience with basic logical thinking. It is a form of reasoning that tries to minimize the uncertainty about the future. This mental processing also occurs when some things just jump out at you in a flash of insight. But as I said, these kinds of intuitive analyses do not guarantee success, nor do the programs that analyze 100 variables. We also have to guard against a false premise: thinking that short term success guarantees long-term success. The Hong Kong group disbanded after they won enough to move on to other enterprises, so we do not know whether their success would have extended far into the future.

There are some cautionary tales from the world of money trading that illustrate quite clearly how systems that made billions for investors quickly turned into massive losses. The mistaken belief that their winning streak guaranteed future success spelled their eventual doom. The Greeks long ago wrote about hubris, and how human arrogance is punished by the gods.

How long did you stay in Florida?

Around two years. During that time I learned a lot about creating my own database. Many of the books I read offered flawed systems which were easily revealed by simply applying them to hypothetical bets, so no actual money needed to be invested. I eventually realized that I needed to take time off to refresh my mind. Sometimes too much close attention focused on one race track led to second-guessing, overthinking, and placing emphasis on what should have been a minor point. I managed to squeak out enough to pay expenses, but not a profit. I also learned the importance of not trying to win a set amount every day because losing streaks are inevitable. When starting out, it is much better to keep track of weekly wins and losses, and then expand to monthly wins and losses. But I had already realized that you cannot bet every race and expect to win in the long run.

Why not?

Simply because good handicapping should reveal those races where you have a better chance of winning. If you analyze a race and you determine that there are no standout horses, then skipping the race is prudent. One fellow I knew bet races that were run only over a fast track. He was so rigorous in his behavior that even if it just sprinkled rain, he went home. Some people make specific types of races their sole focus, such as betting only turf races or maiden races. Other people focus on the trainers, so they study the races a particular trainer does well at, such as getting young horses to run, or doing exceptionally well at training turf horses.

I learned many important things about gambling from people I chanced to encounter. One was told to me by a poker player who said that since you cannot win every hand you must not try to win every hand. You should wait for the right opportunity. He said that he would often sit down at a poker table and drop out of hands for over an hour until he felt like an opportunity presented itself to bet. The same goes for horse racing. The idea is to wait for a race where your analysis gives you confidence to make a bet. Confidence does not guarantee success; it simply allows you to say that you made the best decision in an uncertain situation. As I said, I arrived at that insight from talking to several people along the way. The person who most impressed me was an old horse racing fellow who had the most patience I ever saw. He could go to the track every day for a week and not make a bet. His decision to bet, even if he lost, was made on the basis of his best assessment; otherwise, he said, why bet?

> *I see his point. I don't know if I would have that much patience to wait so long to make a bet, especially if that was meant to be my main source of income.*

It takes a special attitude to achieve that level of patience. He had a calm about him that I admired. Winning or losing never seemed to affect his facial expression. He always maintained a Buddha smile, one that radiates enlightenment and inward peace.

Buddha's smile is captivating. It has an immediate calming effect that beckons you to reassess how you see the world.

Chapter 4

ACTS

Although there are many ways to lose a horse race, some unscrupulous people have figured out how to lose a race but still win. For example, I recall reading about a case involving a major race that had an overwhelming favorite. There was so much money wagered on the favorite with illegal bookies that the bookies would be hit hard having to pay off the bets. So, they devised a simple plan. They found the horse's groom—the person charged with taking care of the horse on a daily basis and who is responsible for staying with the horse the night before the big race—and they offered him a large bribe to make sure that the horse would not win the race.

I hope he didn't have to hurt the horse.

The bookies wanted the horse to run in the race, but not win, so they could keep all the money bet on the favorite. Their plan was amazingly simple. All the groom had to do was make sure the horse did not get much sleep the night before the race. The groom merely had to keep waking the horse every time it began to fall asleep. By the time of the race the lack of sleep ensured the horse would lose. He ran credibly, but he just did not have enough energy to win. The bookies kept all the money that was bet on the horse, so they had a great day. Not so great for those associated with the horse, and of course, those who bet the favorite.

Maybe that's the result of choosing to bet illegally. Why couldn't they place those bets legally?

Your question raises an important turning point in horse racing history—the advent of simulcast wagering. Sometime in the late 1970s, I forget the exact date, the federal government passed the Interstate Horse racing Act which made interstate wagering on horse racing legal. Before the law was passed, you had to place a bet in person at a racetrack. Of course, you could have someone place a bet for you, if they were willing to go in person. Illegal bookmakers flourished because people wanted to make bets on racetracks that were in other states. The risk being that bookies might not pay off your winning bets, and if so, you had no legal recourse to sue because you engaged in an illegal activity.

The new law allowed states to set up account wagering, which requires bettors to create a personal account into which they can deposit money for betting. The licensed account wagering firm then makes sure that your bets get processed into the total wagering pool across the country, thus ensuring a uniform payout to all bettors. And since the racetracks and the account wagering firms take out a percentage of every bet, after which the remaining pool is divided among the winning bets, the problem that bedeviled illegal bookies did not arise for the legal wagering firms.

Can you explain a bit more about how the percentage works?

Sure. Since the takeout percentage differs depending on the kind of bet and the racing jurisdiction, I will just use some made-up numbers to keep it simple. Imagine that you were taking bets on a race. Now suppose there are ten horses, and each horse gets a different amount bet on it. Again, keeping it simple, suppose the total amount bet is $100. The horse that gets the most money bet on it is the favorite, and it has the lowest odds. The odds are calculated by first making sure that the racetrack's take-out percentage, and the account wagering firm, are subtracted from the $100 pool. The take-out assures the racetrack and the account wagering firm can pay their operating costs. Suppose the take-out is 20%. That means that $80 is left from the initial $100 betting pool. To calculate the odds, you divide the $80 by the number of tickets bet on each horse. The favorite has the lowest odds because it has the most money bet on it. So, no matter which horse wins, the total amount paid out is $80, which means that you, as the person taking the bets, keep $20.

That seems straightforward. It protects the racetrack, the account wagering firms, and the bettors because they are assured of getting paid.

Correct. I recall another story about the pre-simulcasting days. It involved a small group who thought of a way to manipulate the odds in their favor, but it did not involve illegal bookies. Long before recent federal legislation allowed states to regulate different forms of gambling, Nevada had been the only state that had legalized gambling, including taking bets on horse racing. If you wanted to make legal bets, you could go to Las Vegas, but that was not an option for most people. A group of gamblers thought of a way to exploit the system in Nevada. Imagine you were visiting Las Vegas and you wanted to bet a race in New York. The casino took your bet and, if your horse won, you were paid the same amount as the New York race track. But since this was before simulcasting and pooled betting, the casino acted as a legal bookie, meaning that they were solely responsible for paying out any winning bets.

To understand how the group was able to exploit this system, you need to understand how local betting pools work. There are big racetracks, such as Aqueduct and Belmont in New York, and Santa Anita and Del Mar in California, that take in millions of dollars in bets, sometimes on a single race. But there are some small race tracks around the country that take in only a few thousand dollars on a race.

I explained earlier how the payoffs are determined by how much money is bet on each horse. But now we need to expand that to see how various bets are possible. Betting to "win" on a horse means that the only way you collect is if your horse comes in first. That wager has its own separate pool of money. Suppose you are not completely confident that your horse will win, but you think that maybe it will come in at least second. If so, then you can bet the horse to "place," meaning that if it comes in either first or second, then you collect. That wager also has its own separate pool of money. An even safer bet is a "show" bet, meaning that if it comes in either first, second, or third, then you collect. And once again, that wager has its own separate pool of money.

Why wouldn't you always bet to show? That way you have three chances to collect.

You are right, but there is a drawback. Again, to keep things simple, disregard the possibility of horses crossing the finish line at the same time, this is called a "dead heat." Given this stipulation, there is normally one horse that comes in first, and the number of tickets bet on this horse determines how much each ticket is worth. For example, if the favorite wins, then the payoff is usually quite small because there are a lot of winning tickets. If a horse is "even money" or 1:1, then if you bet $2, the usual minimum bet at race tracks, then you get back $4, for a profit of $2.

Now observe what happens for a place bet. Recall that a place bet means that if your horse comes in either first or second, then you collect. So, unlike the win bet, there are two payoffs because one horse came in first, another horse came in second, and all the place bets get paid. The result is that the place pool of money has to get divided among more tickets, so the payouts are generally lower than the win bet which pays out for only one horse. For example, suppose you bet the favorite to place. You have to share the place pool money with people who bet the second horse to place. This generally results with the favorite paying around $2.60 for a $2 place bet, for a 60-cent profit.

Payouts get even smaller for show bets for the same reason. Recall that a show bet pays out for the horses that came in first, second, and third. Again, since this is a separate betting pool of money, there are lots of tickets that need to be paid. This is why favorites, for example, pay around $2.20 for a show bet, for a 20-cent profit on a $2 bet.

So although you have a greater chance of collecting a show bet than a win bet, the payout is much smaller.

Yes, and since your profit margin is so small for each show bet, a few losing bets severely hurts your overall bottom line.

I see. It looked like betting to show was an easy way to win money.

There are some statistical regularities in horse racing. For example, historical data shows that for nearly all race tracks in the United States, the favorite wins around one-third of the time. And they are "in the money," meaning they come in either first, second, or third, around two-thirds of the time. This is quite remarkable if you consider probabilities. Suppose there are ten pieces of paper in a box where each piece has a number from 1-10 written on it, and no two pieces have the same number. In a random draw, each piece has a one-in-ten chance of being picked, or 10%. No matter how many times you play this game, the chances of any one number being picked remains the same. After millions of games each number will be near to the 10% mark.

Compare that with horse racing. Imagine there are ten horses in each horse race. Of course, real races can have more or fewer than ten, but we want to simplify things. Each race has a betting favorite. If this were like the pieces-of-paper game, then the favorite would be expected to perform no better than the other horses. But, as I said, favorites win around 33% of the time. This means that horse races are not completely random events. And favorites are in the money around 66% of the time.

Can those statistics be exploited by smart gamblers?

There are reports of some gambling syndicates having used advanced programming techniques that can take advantage of "economic irregularities" in betting pools, but I do not know enough about that to offer an opinion. I am aware of situations where people or groups have tried to use show bets to their advantage. Since the favorite is in the money 66% of the time, and since the show payoff is so small, those bettors place large wagers on the favorite to show, often a million dollars.

That seems smart. They have a good chance of collecting.

We have to look at how it can play out. With that much money in the show pool, the payout will most likely be $2.10, the minimum allowed payout. Therefore, the winning payout for the million dollar bet will amount to a $50,000 profit.

That's not bad considering how short the wait is for the profit. It's hard to get five percent profit on a long-term investment.

Granted, but consider the downside. If you lose, that is a million dollars lost on one bet. It would take only one lost bet like that to wipe out any profit for other similar bets. You would have to win twenty bets at one million dollars each to get back your million dollar loss. Not surprisingly, bettors who lose these kinds of bets are called "bridge jumpers."

Have you seen these kinds of bets?

Oh yes, many times. When you watch the simulcasts, the win, place, and show pools are displayed periodically before the race goes off. If you are physically at the racetrack, the infield tote board displays those three pools all the time before the race goes off. It is fascinating to see those bets appear on the board, and it adds another layer of excitement as you watch the race unfold.

This was a long and winding road from where we started. I was telling you about the group who manipulated the Nevada betting system before simulcasting and the advent of combined betting pools.

I forgot about that. Please go on.

It relies on what I said earlier about why favorites pay so little for a show bet because most of the money has been bet on it. The betting group in question knew that small tracks around the country have small betting pools, so their plan revolved around that simple fact. An average show pool at a small track for all the horses in a single race might be less than $1000, because before simulcasting the only money bet at a small track was from those who physically went to the track, perhaps as few as a couple of hundred people. But no matter the attendance, the favorite in the show pool was most likely going to pay around $2.10. The group knew that if they bet a large amount of money on any horse in a given race at a small track, then that horse would be the favorite. They handicapped each race looking for two things:

a horse most likely to win or at least be in the money in a given race, and a horse most likely to not finish in the money in that same race.

Let's see if I understand this so far. The horse most likely to win a given race will be the favorite, and a horse most likely to not finish in the money will be a long shot.

Right. Of course, this depends on how the betting public sees the race. But regular race goers usually make the most likely candidate the betting favorite.

Okay, good. But I don't see how that helps the group. The favorite will still have the smallest payout.

Correct again. But here is where the scheme famously exploited that fact. Recall that each betting pool—win, place, and show—are separate pools, so each pool's payoff is dependent solely on the amount of money and the number of tickets bet into that individual pool. In most instances the favorite in the win pool also has the most money bet on it in the place pool, and the show pool as well.

That makes sense. The same people who bet the favorite to win probably bet to place and show to get some money back in case the favorite comes in second or third.

Correct. But this group saw something that others missed. Suppose they have someone at the local small racetrack bet $1000 to show on a horse most likely to not finish in the money. That horse will end up having far more tickets on it in the show pool than any other horse in the race, including the horse that is the favorite in the win pool. The idea behind the scheme was that since the least likely horse to finish in the money will probably not run first, second, or third, then all the money bet on it, including the group's $1000, will now be distributed among the first three finishers. Given this outcome, a win pool favorite that normally would pay out a show bet at $2.10 might pay out $6 or more. That was the first half of the plan. The second half required some members of the group to be in Las Vegas. Those bettors would then go to several casinos and spread out a lot of money to show, say $10,000, on the horse they figured would most likely come in the money, usually the win pool favorite. The casino would have to pay the full track payout for the show bet. In our hypothetical case, the on-track bet was $1000, which they were willing to lose, in order to cash $10,000 worth of tickets on a horse that should have paid $2.10, but instead paid $6, for a total payout of $30,000 from the casinos.

That was clever. I now see why they were able to manipulate the existence of separate betting pools at a small track, so Las Vegas casinos had to pay whatever the track paid out. And I also see why simulcasting and the merging of betting pools around the country eliminated that group's scheme.

Yes it did. But I imagine they had fun while it lasted. There are many stories recounting the extent that people will go to win money.

Don't they run the risk of being caught?

Yes, of course. But sometimes the penalty is not enough to deter the culprits. Every once in a while a trainer or jockey is suspended from racing. For trainers, it often stems from using prohibited drugs on their horses. For jockeys, it can result from their causing interference in a race by having their horse intentionally block another horse, or from using a "buzzer," a device that uses small batteries to shock their horse to cause it to run faster. Many of the suspensions are for a few weeks or months, but in rare cases someone is suspended for years. The flip side of trying to maximize the chances of your horse winning are the schemes devised to maximize the chances of it losing.

Why would anyone want their horse to lose a race?

The amount of money that the winners get in many places is usually quite small, at times perhaps a few thousand dollars at the smaller tracks. This leads to manipulating a race to win money by betting. For example, a common scheme involves horses that have won a few races in a row. These were likely to be the favorites in an upcoming race, which meant that anyone betting on them would not win much. But if you knew that the favorite was going to lose, then you can get high odds on the other logical contenders. Trainers and jockeys can collude to do things to ensure their horse would not win, such as having the jockey make sure the horse does not break fast from the gate, thus causing the horse to run from behind the others. Similarly, a jockey can place his horse behind several others who are in a position to block the horse through most of the race. Some jockeys have even intentionally fallen off their horse right after the start, and although that can be dangerous, it assures that their horse will not win.

Those things sound horribly corrupt. My goodness, those people should be sent to prison.

As I said, they are rarely punished enough to affect their behavior or that of others. The role of punishment in criminal theory seems to be driven by emotions. For example, humans have developed four main justifications for punishing criminals. (1) Retribution, commonly referred to as "revenge," or even more commonly called "an eye for an eye." (2) Rehabilitation, the attempt to reform the character or behavior of criminals, so they can become useful and non-threatening members of society. (3) Incapacitation, simply removing criminals by placing them in prison, so they cannot harm members

70

of society. (4) Deterrence, the attempt to discourage others from committing crimes.

The theory behind the concept of deterrence was spelled out clearly by Cesare Beccaria, who lived in the 1700's. Beccaria wrote a short, influential book, *On Crimes and Punishments,* in which he provided a foundation for the concept of deterrence. The bedrock position for Beccaria was the idea that there is only one logical justification for punishment—the rational desire for humans to create a better society. Given this, Beccaria argued that deterrence was the only logically justified course of action. Once deterrence is accepted as the best option, Beccaria argued further that, in order for it to function correctly, efficiently, and effectively, we have to apply two basic principles. The first is "certainty," the idea that we must ensure that all members of society clearly and readily see and understand that the laws are strictly enforced and that punishment is consistently applied. This means that identical punishments have to be applied to identical crimes.

But that's not how sentencing seems to be applied today. I mean judges often have wide discretion to apply sentences to those found guilty.

And it is for just that reason that Beccaria argued that judges should not be given the power to set punishments. This follows from his first principle; if judges are allowed to set different punishments for the same crime, then certainty is nullified, and deterrence neutered.

Beccaria's second principle is "celerity," the idea that punishment must occur swiftly. Beccaria argued that the members of society not only need to connect a specific punishment to a specific crime—that is the first principle, certainty—they also need the connection to happen as quickly as possible—this is the second principle, celerity. Beccaria said that "A punishment may not be an act of violence, of one, or of many, against a private member of society; it should be public, immediate, and necessary, the least possible in the case given, proportioned to the crime, and determined by the laws."

Beccaria also argued something that is quite relevant to today's societies, and something that has become apparent in affluent countries. He said that the most damaging crimes are committed by those who have gained the greatest benefits from society.

You mean white-collar crimes.

Yes. Although Beccaria wrote his book over two hundred years ago, his ideas capture the outrage that many people have for the way that the rich, the famous, and the powerful are often punished for their criminal behavior. When we see wealthy and well-connected criminals abusing their positions in society for personal gain, and getting ridiculously light punishments, the fragile fabric of society is shredded. Sorry to have gone on such a tangent, but it just seemed to flow from our discussion of the lack of punishment for those who abuse systems for their own monetary gain.

> *I'm beginning to see how Beccaria's ideas might help to deter these kinds of criminal behavior. Are there other cases?*

Sure. I remember reading about an intimidating and dangerous ploy by some bookies who did not want a certain favorite to win the next day's major stakes race. They broke into the car of the jockey scheduled to ride the horse, placed a bullet on the front seat, along with a note that said if he won the race, then the next bullet would be coming directly at his head at a much faster speed.

> *Wow, that was awful.*

It is amazing how many ways people have thought of doing harm. If only they had focused their energy and intellect toward helping others, there is no telling how better off we would all be. The ability to harm is amplified by brains that have evolved to solve complex problems and that have the ability to think of unlimited possibilities. To paraphrase—and take a quote out of context just to fit the idea of people doing awful things just to get ahead—Bertrand Russell, a British philosopher, said that misdeeds like these have all the advantages of theft over honest work.

Bringing it back to punishment, theft does have the advantage over honest work, unless it is punished.

Yes, I suspect that the possibility of punishment does factor into some people's decisions whether or not to commit a crime, but perhaps deterrence has certain limitations, one being that the crime is rational.

What do you mean?

Although many crimes are thought out ahead of time, crimes of passion usually are not. The threat of punishment, no matter how certain and swift, is not likely to deter someone who commits a crime as the result of an immediate emotional response to a situation. In contrast, rational crimes are those where the criminal spends some time planning the act.

What measures does horse racing have in place to stop the cheating?

A major problem for a long time was the lack of a universal system of rules or a central governing body to oversee racing. A trainer or jockey who was suspended in one state could simply move to another state because each state had their own racing jurisdiction. Today there is more cooperation between states since they have adopted what is called "reciprocity" whereby rulings issued in one state will be accepted by all other racing jurisdictions. There are exceptions because states have different medication restrictions for use on horses, and different timelines when those medications can be used on a horse. So, a trainer might be suspended in one state for violating that state's medical rules, but be allowed to run his horses in another state where the rules are different. There is work being done toward having a federal body of rules and a regulating agency which, if adopted, will be a good thing. But until that happens each state has its own system of rules and enforcement mechanisms. Trainers and jockeys are fined and suspended, but they have the right to appeal the decisions which can drag out for months or even years—which is the opposite of Beccaria's idea of celerity. Theoretically, punishment should be a disincentive to specific acts.

What do you mean by "theoretically?"

If we use Beccaria's ideas about deterrence, then the punishment should fit the crime in the sense that it is swift and certain. But there must also be a price to pay that makes the disincentive such that the perpetrators will not simply resume their corrupt behavior. A small fine will not dissuade someone who is already making a lot of money from the behavior, nor will a short suspension affect much either. Someone who is rewarded by bad behavior, such as a trainer who is allowed to continue training horses even when "punished" by a state racing commission, and who is supported by horse owners who are interested only in winning, will continue to thrive in the business. Trainers are judged by how often their horses win, so the incentive for them to win at all costs is usually far greater than the disincentive for getting caught.

It's the lack of severe or at least adequate punishment that affects the bottom-line of trainers, owners, and jockeys that allows the corruption to exist.

That is a big part of it. We know that humans are affected by incentives and disincentives, by rewards, and punishments. But we seem to focus only on one side of the question, the external part.

What do you mean?

There is a vast difference between an external incentive and an internal incentive. Likewise, for an external disincentive and an internal disincentive. External incentives are inducements to act a certain way because of some external reward; for example, money or material goods. In contrast, internal incentives are personal characteristics or virtues that define the person. Someone might say, "I will act in a way that benefits society, not because I can get something, but because it is the right thing to do, and I want to be an honest person. My actions define my character." This internal concern is with "What sort of person do I want to be" rather than the external concern with "What can I get from my actions?" or "What's in it for me?"

For some reason it doesn't seem as if the internal incentive to be a good person outweighs the potential external incentives for most people. And since we already saw that external disincentives are often not adequate for deterrence, then how can internal disincentives possibly work to motivate behavior?

I am open to suggestions.

Wait, you expect me to figure it out?

Why not? You are as capable as anyone else. Perhaps Socrates would say that if you are capable of understanding the question, then you are capable of figuring out the answer. Socrates thought that our first priority should be the development of our character, so his concern was internal. The idea is that if you strive for wisdom, self-control, and temperance in your needs, then your outward behavior will always be on the right track. Our internal nature guides our external relations, so good character leads to good intentions.

I thought the road to hell was paved with good intentions.

It may be, but that is because of the uncertainty involved in our lives. Good intentions can lead to bad outcomes, and bad intentions can lead to good outcomes. Nevertheless, perhaps our moral decisions and actions are similar to our practical decisions, that is, guided by what we have learned through personal experience and history. To think that unless every decision we make in a world of uncertainty has to turn out right is to chase after the illusion of certainty in the physical world.

Somehow knowing that doesn't make the problems any easier.

I trust that when you bought your train ticket this morning you did not expect that all questions of life would be answered. A pleasant train ride is perhaps all we can hope for.

The internal and external discussion can be used to understand some moral theories. The German philosopher, Immanuel Kant, spelled out the case for the role of duty. Kant held that moral directives are derived from our ability to reason. He defined a "categorical imperative" as a rule of conduct, an unconditional and universal obligation to act in a certain way. In simple terms, "categorical" means absolute, and "imperative" means obligation, so we are under absolute obligations to act in certain ways, no matter the consequences.

In contrast, utilitarianism emphasizes the consequences of our actions; the greatest happiness of the greatest number of people should be the guiding principle of our conduct. We must weigh our actions and act accordingly. The term can be understood in its application to the social benefits of public utilities, which are meant to benefit everyone in society.

A third idea, virtue ethics, places emphasis on individual virtues, our moral character. For example, if you help someone in need without any expectation of an external reward for your action, then this reveals your moral character.

Those are strong points, and they seem to make sense in certain cases, but none seems to fit all the possible moral decisions we can face.

True, each has strong and weak spots. For example, Kant's categorical imperatives face a problem: How do you reconcile conflicting duties? For example, the duty to tell the truth with the duty to protect someone from harm. Perhaps one way out is to judge which action will cause the least harm. But then we would be looking at the consequences of our actions, which is not what we are supposed to do according to Kant's theory. But if we sometimes cannot ignore the consequences of our actions, then perhaps we need to reconcile utilitarianism with the role of duties.

I recall a situation where three friends and I were trying to agree on where we should eat. Three of us wanted to eat at one place and one voted for another place. Although we didn't use the term utilitarianism, we three argued that the group as a whole would derive more pleasure if we went to

79

the place of our choice rather than the choice of the dissenting person. Upon which the dissenting person remarked that the principle we were using was that the selfishness of three should outweigh the selfishness of one.

That is a great story. And perhaps a virtue ethicist might say that the group of three would have revealed their inner benevolent nature if they all went along with the one dissenter. Of course, if our decisions should always be based on our good intentions, then we run into a problem. We have direct access to physical actions, but not to intentions, other than taking someone's word for it. Granted that bad results can come from good intentions, but that reduces our moral judgment to something we cannot objectively observe, the intention. Seeking to be virtuous is both an internal and external activity. Socrates urges us to nurture our virtues—for example, being honest and just towards others—but our actions are what we observe and they are the basis for others saying that someone is virtuous, or dangerous, because we are forced to interpret her actions, we cannot see her internal character. Socrates maintains that we should not expect that our internal virtues will guarantee beneficial results in all our actions toward others, because that assumes that we can predict the future with certainty.

Chapter 5

RINGS

Plato wrote something that we can apply to the discussion of internal and external incentives. In one of the dialogues, Socrates is asked a simple question by his friend Glaucon: "Why should we be good?" Although Glaucon believes we should be good, he is disturbed by a story about human nature that argues we should be evil. The story is about Gyges, a shepherd who found a ring that enables its wearer to become invisible. The power to become invisible corrupted Gyges and led him to commit terrible acts, such as killing the King and assuming absolute power.

That sounds like the movie, The Lord of the Rings.

It has been speculated that Tolkien was influenced by Plato's Ring of Gyges story, but I did not look into the evidence for or against the speculation. The basic idea of a ring of invisibility is the same in both stories.

I might look into that. But please continue.

Glaucon continues the story and asks us to suppose that two rings exist, where one was found by a just person and the other by an unjust person. Does anyone think that sooner or later the just person would not be corrupted? The realization that you would never be caught would be too strong a temptation for even a just person. The just person might start wielding the power for what he considers good ends, even though it might entail committing bad acts to achieve his ends.

> *The temptation would be too much for anyone, especially since you would never be caught. You know, this seems like what happens when people use the anonymity of the internet to write horrible things, or to commit acts thinking they will never get caught. I recall reading a while back about some fellow who started drug dealing on the dark web, which at the time was not adequately policed. Although his enterprise became world-wide, he was eventually caught. I remember distinctly that he thought the dark web made him invisible. So, Plato's story resonates even today.*

The idea of invisibility as a corrupting power is what worried Glaucon, and why he hoped Socrates could alleviate his concern. The argument is that such power is so great that even a just person will eventually succumb. If this is right, then perhaps we are not willingly good people; we are good only out of fear of being punished for doing wrong. If this is right, then since the ring eliminates the fear of being punished, we are free to be evil. Anyone obtaining the power, but not using it for personal gain at the expense of others, would be considered a fool. But Glaucon's story is not finished. Suppose a person not only wants to appear to be a good person, he wants to be a good person.

I don't think I understand.

This is what we are calling the external and internal parts of us; the appearance of being good versus having an internal good character. Imagine two people, one just and the other unjust. And imagine that the just person suffers throughout his life, but the unjust person lives a life of luxury. At their hour of death, who shall we say had the happier life? That is the question Glaucon poses to Socrates.

> *I see the importance of distinguishing the external life of appearance from the internal life of character. That's quite a challenge to Socrates. I'm not sure I could give Glaucon a satisfactory answer, so I'm anxious to hear what Socrates said.*

It is quite a challenge. Socrates has to show that being a just person is better than being an unjust person. He also has to consider how our external and internal selves are impacted by our actions, especially since we can see only the outward appearance of someone, not their inner character.

I guess that's why we say actions speak louder than words. But even my best intentions may backfire when I act. If so, then how can I prove that my intentions are pure and my character is virtuous? It sure looks like all we have access to are each other's actions. But that's a lousy result. I'm not happy with that.

Socrates admitted that the story of Gyges led to a strong argument that outward appearance, a life of external happiness, seems to be more important than internal goodness. And for most people, since the fear of punishment is a strong deterrent to bad behavior, perhaps that is the only reason why people are good, and why the ring releases us from the fear of punishment.

Socrates begins his answer by asking us to think of an image of a complex creature made up of three distinct inner parts. First, a many-headed wild monster; second, a lion; and third, a human. Next, have the outward appearance be that of a human. But since no one can see the three inner parts, all we see is a single human form.

That's a strange image, but I think I have it.

This is where Socrates wants us to think about our inner nature, our character, or soul, if you prefer that term. If the argument for being evil while never being exposed is correct, then the creature should release the many-headed wild monster and lion to get what it wants, and suppress the human part. But we can ask someone who holds this position to consider the following: A person who strives only for outward gain and pleasure might sell his child or other family members into slavery for money. If so, would his outward gain enrich his inward character? And as the thirst for outward gain can never be fully satisfied, the inner beasts grow larger and stronger, leading to ever more horrible acts and the suffering of others.

But those things don't seem to dissuade, or even bother, evil people and those who seek power and riches. You can't reason with some people, so how can we get them to change?

It may not be possible for everyone, short of genetic manipulation or behavioral feedback training, which would have to be defended by moral arguments. For example, if we do those things, then we would have to justify physically altering a person's character by the ends which we desired to bring about. The book, *A Clockwork Orange*, by Anthony Burgess, does a good job of presenting this idea, and the Stanley Kubrick movie adaptation of the book contains a stunning visual representation of it.

But for Socrates, the fight is an internal one. We each have to fight our inner beasts through reason, since that is the only gateway to truth and wisdom.

Because an evil person is a slave to his unquenchable desires, Socrates argues that it is better to be ruled by reason than by pleasure and power, because wisdom lasts far longer than temporary pleasure and power.

> *Socrates has a way of putting things that make them sound reasonable, but maybe his words resonate with people who already lean his way. I mean, the world around us is chock full of narcissistic, power hungry, greedy, unscrupulous people who act like they will never be stopped, so maybe there are a lot of rings going around.*

You may be right. If so, we need to find out where they are made and sold. Check the dark web. Socrates's position relies on a belief that all humans are capable of reason, without which his arguments would fail. Modern psychology seems to suggest that may not be true. For example, if by "reason" we mean having a social conscience, then psychopaths and sociopaths seem to lack that characteristic.

The idea of corruption presented by the ring of Gyges story runs through a lot of literature. For example, Goethe's *Faust*, depicts a man who was willing to sell his soul in return for knowledge and pleasure. And Robert Louis Stevenson's *Strange Case of Dr. Jekyll and Mr. Hyde*, depicts the dual personality of the main character. And Oscar Wilde's *The Picture of Dorian Gray*, shows the main character wanting to live a life of pleasure, but also wanting never to age. In that story, Dorian's portrait not only ages, it becomes hideous through his acts.

> *Socrates's belief is that although your bad acts may not affect your outer life, the external part of you, your bad acts will corrupt your inner life, which for Socrates is the essential part of us.*

Yes, that is Socrates's position.

Chapter 6

ABSURDITIES

Can we bring in a related idea? Isn't religion a necessary ingredient in moral arguments? Who said that if God didn't exist then everything would be permitted?

There is a passage in Dostoyevsky's *The Brothers Karamazov* that has that sentiment. Many people have paraphrased the passage throughout the years. Although it is possible to live a moral life with religious beliefs, it is equally possible to live a moral life without religious beliefs. So, no, religion is not a necessary ingredient to moral arguments. Arthur Clarke wrote the following: "The greatest tragedy in mankind's entire history may be the hijacking of morality by religion."

There is an often used argument technique called *reductio ad absurdum,* which means reduction to an absurdity, It is used extensively by philosophers and mathematicians. On the one hand, suppose you want to prove that your claim about something is correct. You can start by assuming the negation, the opposite, of your claim. If you derive a contradiction, then the assumption must be false. But since your assumption was the opposite of your claim, you have shown that your original claim must be correct.

On the other hand, suppose you wanted to show that someone else's claim was incorrect. This time you assume that it is true and then try to derive a contradiction. If you can successfully derive a contradiction, then you have shown that the person's claim was incorrect. In both cases, the technique works when an initial assumption is refuted by showing that it leads to a contradiction, in other words, an absurdity.

There are several types of arguments for the existence of God. A cosmological argument starts by assuming that something exists, say the universe. It is a safe bet that most people would not object to this assumption; but notice I said "most people." It is then assumed that everything that exists has a cause. Given these two assumptions, the argument concludes that it is necessary that something must exist to cause the universe to exist, namely God.

But if the cause and effect assumption is correct, then how can it stop? There will always need to be another cause, so it can't end.

You raise a salient point. The second assumption—every effect has a cause—seems to lead to an infinite regress, a series that never ends. It is here that most arguments invoke a description of God as the first cause. The description relies on the characteristics generally attributed to God, namely, an omnipotent, omniscient, and eternal being.

That seems to be cheating. Why can't the universe come from nothing, or why not assume that the universe is itself eternal? That way no God is needed.

You have articulated a common criticism of the "first cause" argument. Since any argument we devise, no matter its topic, requires some assumptions to get started, it is perfectly appropriate to challenge some or all of those assumptions.

A related argument for the existence of God is called the "argument by analogy." Several versions have been offered, such as the "intelligent design argument," but they have a common core. The idea goes like this: If the universe has order, then it must have been designed. The universe has order, thus, it must have a designer, namely God who has the characteristics mentioned earlier. This is an analogical argument that relies on a specific assumption: things that share certain characteristics most likely share other characteristics. We accept that a watch cannot arise from a random series of events; therefore, it has to have a designer, a creator. And since the universe has design, it has a designer, it was created by God.

But the universe is not really like a watch. I mean, granted it has some order, but it also has a lot of disorder, and it unfolds in many unpredictable ways.

You sound like David Hume, a famous British philosopher. Hume said that objects that we create are different from the universe which displays a lot of randomness. Hume also argued that even though we can see some order, such as plant and animal life, we know that they are the result of natural processes that need no intentional designer to bring them about. But Hume was not finished with his criticism. He applied the reductio ad absurdum technique by arguing that if the design argument was correct, then since watches are created by finite creatures, perhaps God is finite. Since we are imperfect creatures, then maybe God is imperfect. Groups of people create watches, so maybe a group of gods were needed to create the universe.

That's good. Since the argument for God relies on the force of an analogy, Hume uses the original assumptions to create some absurd results.

There are many arguments for God's existence, but none has proven to be acceptable to everyone. There is a story about this never-ending search. A philosopher once gave a talk where he claimed that although every argument for God's existence is flawed, the sheer number of such arguments should be enough to persuade us that God exists. Upon which the philosopher, I think it was Sidney

Morgenbesser, said that if one dead horse cannot pull a wagon, then maybe twenty dead horses can do it.

That's clever. Perhaps some philosophers are comedians.

That is a good observation, and one we might pursue later, if we have time. But just as a quick follow-up, a colleague of mine said that although the wagon won't move an inch when attached to the twenty dead horses, perhaps the wagon might appreciate the effort.

When it comes to believing in God, Søren Kierkegaard said that since God is the great unknown that will forever escape our powers of reason, our struggle to prove God's existence is futile. Therefore, belief in the existence of God rests ultimately on a leap of faith.

Chapter 7

APPLICATIONS

Although I want to continue with these philosophical discussions, it just occurred to me that we left off talking about what happened when you began to pursue a gambling career. Do you mind going back to that?

Not at all. I think we left off when I spent time in south Florida. I enjoyed living there but I got restless and decided to give Las Vegas a try since the casinos offered easy access to horse racing betting across the country through simulcasting. It also provided the opportunity for an in-depth exploration of many different games of chance. But I still continued to concentrate on horse racing. Once again, I was able to keep my head above water as far as finances were concerned, but—

Wait, don't tell me. You got restless again.

Correct. After three years in Vegas, I got the itch to try something new. I had just turned 30, so I decided to try applying to graduate schools. If I did not get in, then I would either keep trying the horse racing game, or switch to poker. I knew getting accepted was a long-shot, but since I had experience with taking chances and dealing with uncertainty, it was a gamble I thought worth taking.

I knew there were many variables that would affect my getting accepted, so I began by listing those that I could control and those I could not. For example, graduate schools typically require letters of recommendation from professors who are familiar with your academic achievement and potential for graduate school. When I graduated with a bachelor's degree I did not ask any of my teachers to write letters because I was not sure if I would ever need them. It was now too late to ask anyone because I did not think those few who knew me would remember much, if anything, about me. The lack of letters in support was a big hole in my application, but I thought that the selection committees might notice my age and perhaps not hold it against me. A second variable that I could not control was my GPA. I mentioned that it was barely over 3.0. I thought that since I was applying to philosophy departments, and since my grades for all my philosophy courses were either A's or B's, then once again the committees might place more weight on that than my overall GPA.

Then I considered the variables over which I had some control. For example, I was expected to submit a Graduate Records Examination, a GRE, score. I signed up and studied a bit, but at that time it tested mostly math and English comprehension skills, so I felt there was not a whole lot I could do to beef up my skills in a short time. Most students take the GRE in their senior year while basic skills are probably at their peak, but that was not available to me anymore.

If you don't mind my asking, how did you do on the exam?

It was a long time ago, so I do not recall my actual score, but I judged that it was barely adequate for the schools I had picked out. What helped immensely was something that I had not known existed. Along with my GRE score, the Educational Testing Service offered booklets for every graduate school discipline throughout the United States. For example, I could buy a booklet that had information about every philosophy department that offered advanced degrees. The information specified whether a department offered a terminal master's degree, or if it offered a PhD as well. It also had information about the average number of students that applied each year to each school, how many were accepted, and how many scholarships, teaching assistantships, and other financial aid that was offered.

I didn't know that information existed. That's important information, and every student should take advantage of it.

It is crucial to have such information, especially considering how much time is spent deciding where to apply, and not knowing how many students are applying. But sadly, the GRE people decided to stop offering the booklets. I learned this when my son began thinking of graduate school.

Do you know why they stopped offering it?

When we could not find anything on the Educational Testing Service website, I called them. The person I talked to had never heard of the booklets, so it must have been discontinued quite some time ago. She was curious and asked if I could explain what the booklets contained. While I was listing all the features she kept saying, "Why don't we offer that anymore?" She said that she would have loved to have such information when she was contemplating graduate school, and that she was going to talk to the people who had been employed there the longest to see if anyone remembered the booklets, and why they were stopped.

I hope your phone call started an internal discussion among the GRE people to perhaps return to creating the booklets.

I hope so, too. The information in the booklet offered a way for me to have a lot of enlightened control over where I would apply. For example, I quickly realized that I should eliminate all the schools that offered both a Master's degree and PhD in philosophy, since they probably expected their applicants to pursue a PhD and to not stop after they earned a Master's degree. This narrowed my search to those schools that offered only a Master's degree. I was also able to narrow the search even more by selecting schools that had a high acceptance rate. I was able to get my search down to two schools, so I sent away for applications.

What do you mean that you had to send away for applications? Couldn't you just email them or download the applications? Oh, wait a minute, this was long before those things were available. Sorry.

It is quite all right. It does seem hard to believe that it took longer to accomplish what today is instantaneous. I had to write letters to request the applications, and write letters and send checks to get my undergraduate transcript and GRE scores sent. It took time for back-and-forth mail to arrive, so the entire process took several months.

Then an unexpected thing happened. I heard back from one of the departments that I was accepted into their program, and although I did not apply for any scholarships or teaching assistantships, TA's, they had a TA position that went unfilled because they did not have enough students who applied that year.

Why hadn't you applied for those?

Two reasons. First, I had saved enough money to allow me to pay all school and living expenses for at least two years. Second, I considered that having been out of school for so long I was not qualified to be a TA, or to get a scholarship. In fact, the prospect of jumping in and being a TA seemed so daunting that I nearly turned it down. But I eventually decided that it would be a good test of whether or not I was fit to do graduate work, so I accepted the offer. And good thing because the other school turned me down.

You were lucky.

The word "luck" makes sense in this instance, but perhaps we can talk about that important concept at a later time, because after dealing with chance situations for most of my life, I like to see how other people understand that concept. So, yes, I agree that there was little chance of all this happening—but it did.

In my second year in the program, I asked the professor I was working with as a TA about my acceptance into the program, and how little chance I gave myself. He told me that it was true that not having any letters of recommendation was a drawback, and my overall GPA was not outstanding, nor was my GRE score. But they considered that since I was 30 years old, perhaps the unfocused and unmotivated young person was gone. They also considered that my overall GPA had gone up every year, and I had done well in all my philosophy courses. Given this, they thought I deserved a chance. Years later he confided to me that when I applied there were so few applicants that they had an unfilled TA position, and since they didn't want to lose the funding for the position. that is part of the reason I got accepted.

You must have completed the Master's degree since you said that you retired from teaching philosophy. Did you also get a PhD degree?

That question that will require a lot of unpacking. Part of the answer goes back to when I described my desire to understand the intellectual discussions that occurred in my university courses. I managed to go through different stages of understanding at the undergraduate level, and then at the graduate level.

The graduate level can be broken down into two stages. The first was my entering the Master's program. My immediate goal was to be able to read philosophy on a graduate level and join in class conversations. This I managed to do. One of the courses I took in my first semester started out with the scheduled professor having to miss the first two weeks, so we had another department professor who filled in. He gave us two articles to read, and we were told that we had to write a paper in which we were to critically assess one of the articles on the basis of the arguments in the other article. The idea was to see if we could understand both articles and apply that understanding by creating some original arguments. We were warned that the missing professor was a tough grader, so by all means do not turn the paper in late because he did not accept any excuses.

That was quite a challenge for your first semester, especially having been out of school for so long.

Indeed. I had given myself two years to see if I could make it, but now it looked like I might be finished far sooner. To remain in the program, students had to maintain a B average, so I knew what was awaiting me. I had to read the articles many, many times, so it was a good thing that they were not long, but they were dense.

What do you mean by "dense."

Compacted reasoning. It is when an author writes in a way that is shorthand for his thoughts because he expects the reader to flesh out the missing parts, which is not easy to do. Oh, that reminds me of a story. A philosophy professor told us of her dissertation advisor who was a famous philosopher, and how he wrote articles for journal publication. His method was as follows: First, he writes it so that even an undergraduate philosophy major can understand it. Then he rewrites it. Now you must be a PhD student to understand it. Then he rewrites it again. This time only a few philosophy professors in the world can understand it. Then he rewrites it again. Now only God and the author can understand it. Then he rewrites it one final time.

That's funny. And now I have a good understanding of the term "dense."

Sorry for the detour. I managed to write the paper and handed it in when the regular instructor returned. He kept our papers for a week and when he returned them to us, he announced the name of a class member who received first prize and who was rewarded with a book. To my astonishment, I got second prize, also a book.

You must have been stunned, but extremely proud.

Well, there were only two students in the class. No, I'm kidding. There were around ten. This was another affirmation from a philosophy teacher, and supremely important for me to get it in my first semester. He recruited me to be his TA for the two years I was there, and he also became my thesis advisor. The two years in the Master's program flew by, and I thoroughly enjoyed myself. I also realized that I could think better in warm climates.

What do you mean?

I had always hated cold weather. Growing up in the northeast meant long grey months of cold weather, snow, sleet, digging your car out from under piles of snow, and trying to keep warm. I recall having to walk home from the Post Office after midnight because the buses stopped running during blizzard-like conditions. The hardest part of the walk was crossing a long bridge because the strong freezing wind and the deep snow slowed progress. There were a few times that I was so cold and tired that I just felt like lying down and going to sleep. That is another reason why I accepted the scouting job.

I remember when I became old enough to realize there were parts of the country that did not get snow and cold weather. I asked my parents why we did not live in those places. They said that people of their generation simply stayed where they were born, quite often because that is where jobs were available. I knew that I always felt uncomfortable throughout the winter months, so much so that it intruded on my academic life, from elementary school to college. Some people prefer to be cool, but I prefer to be warm. It is difficult to keep warm in freezing weather because we need so many calories to fuel our bodies. But hot weather does not require so many calories; in fact, all you need to do is stay hydrated, for the most part.

Sorry for the digression. However, it does offer a possible explanation of why I felt so comfortable at the school, and, I believe, how it contributed to my success there. I wrote my thesis in the fourth semester, and submitted it. When your advisor gives you the go-ahead for submission, then you have a strong chance of passing the oral defense, which in my case consisted of my advisor and two other department professors.

Were you afraid of having to face the thesis committee?

I was, but I thought that I knew the material well enough to get through. My advisor told me the secret to passing was to get the people on the committee to debate each other, thereby taking the heat off me. Nevertheless, I was unprepared for the first question, which was, "What relevance does your thesis have to the general public?"

That seems like a question out of left field. What did you say?

I had no idea how to respond. I never expected such a question. After what seemed like an eternity, I asked if we could come back to that question later on. They agreed, and we moved on. The rest of the defense went smoothly. My thesis consisted in the analysis of three related articles, so each of the three committee members took one part and asked me questions. After about an hour and a half, I was told that I had passed. We never came back to the original question, so that was a relief.

Great. Your confidence must have grown after that.

In one sense it did, but in another sense, I still had doubts. Although I thought I did a good job of understanding the three papers I wrote about, I also knew that it was weak in originality. In fact, my thesis advisor confirmed my suspicion when he said that the strength of my thesis was in my understanding of the ideas involved. He also said that

103

sparks of originality could be seen but had not been developed, which was acceptable at that level. He offered encouragement by saying that my time as a PhD student would give me the added background needed to develop the sustained originality necessary to complete a PhD dissertation.

But I worried about not having been able to answer the first question. It seemed that my absorption into the philosophical nuances of the topic made me unable to connect it to life in general. That thought still lingers.

> *I imagine that many professionals have a hard time explaining the relevance of what they do. I imagine a lot of research is purely speculative and never pans out.*

True. And many mathematicians have said that pure mathematics often has no connection to reality, but that does not take away its intrinsic value for those who pursue it.

> *I see what you mean. So what happened after you got the Master's degree? You must have had to apply to different universities because you said your school offered only a Master's degree, is that right?*

Right. I decided to take a year off to think about where I wanted to go. I seriously thought about avoiding cold weather schools, but finally realized that I should apply to the schools that offered a program that fit my interests no matter where they were located. So, I worked for a year at a gas station. I was given the night shift, and since it was usually not busy, this gave me time to read more in preparation for applying to PhD programs.

When I finally started to apply, I narrowed my search once again to two schools. This time I was accepted by both departments. One offered me a TA position which meant grading exams and papers again, but the other offered me a fellowship which meant that I did not have to do any work for my first year. Both programs offered free tuition, so they were equal on that part, and both departments had good reputations in philosophy, so the deciding factor was the fellowship. I could not pass it up.

I have to ask. Were they in warm or cold weather states?

I am happy that you remembered. Alas, they were both in cold weather states.

Then that would prove to be a good test of your hypothesis that you functioned best in warm weather.

Quite right. My being accepted into a Master's program and then a PhD program reminds of another aspect of the role of chance. Recall that I was accepted into a master's degree program partly because not enough students had applied that year. A similar fact involved my acceptance into the PhD program. They received 10 applications for 4 openings. Several candidates did not even have a bachelor's degree in philosophy, so that helped my cause, especially with my having both a bachelor's degree and a Master's degree in philosophy, so my chances were maximized at that school.

Now compare my situation with what students have to endure today. For example, it is quite common for students today to have to apply to around 20 PhD programs because many schools get over 200 applications for an average of 5 slots.

That's incredible. They have around a two percent chance of getting accepted. Is that right?

Right. Today's students face terrible odds. I would never have been accepted into any program in today's environment.

I had no idea that was the case today. It must be terribly disheartening to be rejected so many times. I have to ask—did you complete the PhD degree?

I will let the story play out for a while until I answer that. The first-year fellowship afforded me the luxury of concentrating exclusively on the course material. In addition, I was now taking classes with some students who were already working on their PhD dissertations, so I expected the class discussions and inevitable student presentations in seminars to be at a much higher level than what I had experienced in the Master's program.

I did well in my coursework, and felt comfortable in giving presentations, so my first year went well. In the second year I was offered a TA position since the fellowship was good for only my first year. The professor I worked for allowed me to give some lectures in her undergraduate introductory courses, so that really helped me understand the challenges of teaching, and paved the way to another unexpected occurrence. In the Spring semester of my second year a chance opportunity presented itself. My university was one of three U.S. schools that were asked to set up two-year programs in a Southeast Asia country. The idea was to have the local students take fully accredited courses whose credits would be accepted by U.S. colleges and universities, so the students would have to spend only a few years in the U.S. to finish their bachelor's degrees. It also let the students experience the way American classes were run, and it gave them extra help in becoming more fluent in English.

My TA professor encouraged me to apply for the job, in part because she knew that I liked to travel and wanted to live overseas, and she thought that it would be a good experience for me. I qualified for the position because I already had a Master's degree. I applied for the one philosophy position available, and I had an interview. Although the interview went well, the position was offered to a senior philosophy professor at my school. But at the last minute he decided not to go. There was not enough time to go through another screening and interview process, so I was offered the job.

> *Another turn of good luck. I assume you accepted the position.*

Of course. Although I longed to travel overseas, I never really expected it to happen. I managed to stay there for five years. The time there allowed me to focus not only on teaching, but trying to reach students from a culture different from my own.

> *How did you finish your coursework and dissertation for the PhD?*

I did not finish. But given my restless nature it did not matter. I was able to parlay my teaching experience and Master's degree into positions at several schools.

> *I do recall we talked about the publish or perish requirement, and at that time you said that it was possible to find teaching positions that didn't require you to publish. So that dovetails with your not needing to get the PhD.*

Nothing stopped me from writing philosophy articles or books and submitting them for publication, if I desired to do so. But it was never an itch that I felt compelled to scratch.

Chapter 8

PHILOSOPHIES

It just hit me that we have been talking for a while but I never asked you how you see the field of philosophy. Can you describe it for me?

I would be happy to give you my interpretation of it. Philosophy stimulates our ability to reason through complex issues, to think thoroughly and precisely about many topics, to analyze perennial problems in a consistent, coherent, and comprehensive manner. These skills have lasting effects by providing personal moments of reflection as we go through life. Although philosophy has its own internal areas of study, it is also an intellectual exercise that connects to other academic disciplines. Philosophy nudges us toward an appreciation of diverse ideas, and challenges us to express our ideas in clear and reasonable terms.

Philosophy has a long history, and through the centuries economic trade connected different cultures, so philosophical ideas were transmitted through time and place. Some ideas took hold and others faded away. Reading philosophy is different from reading about science. Most science courses do not spend much time discussing long discarded scientific theories because there is so much new knowledge to impart. But philosophers from every era in history continue to be read because they offer insight into the deepest and most profound questions of life. Notice that I use the term "insight" instead of "answers." We read current science books looking for the best knowledge available about the physical world. But we read philosophy to see how other thinkers analyzed problems that all people have thought about. Although philosophical texts open up new vistas for us to explore, they are not road maps to some promised land. The goal of any philosophy book, or college course in philosophy for that matter, should be to stimulate us to think clearly, to create a desire for further intellectual challenges.

The term "philosophy" derives from two Greek root words: "philo" meaning love, and "sophia" meaning wisdom, so it is often defined as the love of wisdom. That is broad, so it can also be said that philosophy is the quest for knowledge, or the search for truth.

> *But wouldn't that definition also include science?*

Yes, and that illustrates an important aspect of the history of philosophy, and why philosophical ideas can be found in all areas of intellectual activity. The individual scientific disciplines of today can be traced back to philosophy. The term "scientist" was coined in the 1830's by the British philosopher, William Whewell. Before that, those we now call physicists, chemists, and biologists were called "natural philosophers," which meant that they were philosophers who studied the nature of the physical universe. There was no need to have a separate designation for these people until modern scientific advances created separate branches of study and turned the armchair philosophers into full-blown scientists.

As the individual sciences developed specialized methods and technical equipment for acquiring knowledge of a specific part of nature, the fields became quite independent. But since all scientific disciples branched off from philosophy, science still contains fundamental philosophical questions. Nevertheless, some scientists deny that their work has any connection with philosophy. For example, some physicists criticize other theoretical physicists by claiming, for example, that perhaps string theory is philosophy, not physics.

One of my philosophy teachers lamented that the field of philosophy has been shrinking faster and faster. For example, a large part of logic has been absorbed into mathematics, and the philosophy of mind is being taken over by specialized departments of neuroscience and consciousness studies. With all this happening, my teacher joked that when the next branch separates from philosophy, he is going with it.

Even though each field is specialized, many people accept that all knowledge is connected. For example, interdisciplinary studies bring together researchers from separate academic fields in order to reconnect the branches of knowledge.

You mentioned the sciences such as physics and chemistry. But what about areas such as psychology and sociology?

Philosophical ideas are woven into the most recent social science disciplines, such as psychology, anthropology, linguistics, sociology, and political science, to name just a few subjects. Scratch any scientist and you will reveal a philosopher. It is not difficult to see how the branches of knowledge are connected. Here is one example. Suppose you see on the news that a Category 4 hurricane with wind speeds near 150 mph has struck part of the United States. Imagine that hundreds of people were killed. You might have read that hurricanes like this are becoming more common, and that we can expect to experience many more of these in the future. It is natural to ask why this is happening. Most scientists today explain this as the result of climate change caused by, among other things, the use of fossil fuels and the large-scale destruction of forests, especially in tropical areas.

Scientific knowledge that is developed over decades often leads to consensus among the scientific community. But the general public may wonder how the consensus has been reached. The area of philosophy that investigates such questions is called "epistemology," from the root word "episteme" meaning "to know," and the suffix "-logy" meaning "the study of." Epistemology is the study of knowledge. It is not surprising that epistemology is part of what philosophers of science study because they are interested in understanding the foundations and workings of science. Broadly speaking, they want to know what exactly counts as science and scientific knowledge.

They seem like related questions. I mean, if you know the foundations of science, then you must know what makes an activity scientific, right?

Correct. One goal might be to specify the methods that all sciences have in common. Doing this would enable us to demarcate science from, for example, pseudo-science.

And from religion and, I imagine, from art, literature, superstition, and a host of other things.

The religion aspect is quite important. You might recall some of the court challenges that occurred over certain laws in some states. An important case occurred in Pennsylvania in 2005, where the local school district in Dover passed a law requiring any public school in the district that taught Darwin's theory of evolution to also introduce students to "intelligent design" theory. The law was challenged in court as violating the First Amendment to the U.S.

Constitution's prohibition against the establishment of religion. The judge in the case, John Jones, agreed. He ruled that the law was unconstitutional because intelligent design was not a scientific theory; it was simply a disguised version of Christianity.

The trial had many witnesses who talked about what constitutes science, and the judge displayed a fine ability to understand the kinds of arguments and analyses that belong to the philosophy of science. Anyone interested in intellectual ideas should read Judge Jones's ruling; it is easily accessible online. It is clear, astute, and enlightening.

It sounds fascinating. I'll be sure to look into it.

Epistemology and philosophy of science are invested in understanding science. But we can also branch out from the science behind hurricane formation to see connections to other aspects of knowledge. For example, the damage caused by the hurricane might become the subject of legal inquiries involving insurance. While direct hurricane damage to your home is generally covered by your homeowner insurance, flooding that can occur from a hurricane is generally not covered.

That can't be right.

Unfortunately, it is true. Homeowner's insurance policies cover the damage caused by a hurricane's strong wind, but not by the damage caused by the flooding from a hurricane. You have to buy separate flood insurance for that.

Aren't they both considered "Acts of God?"

Acts of God are given the legal term *force majeure* which means superior force. It refers to things outside human control, such as earthquakes, hurricanes, tsunamis, and floods. For insurance purposes, some Acts of God are covered, but some are not. In most cases, hurricane wind is covered, but not damage caused by earthquakes, volcanoes, or floods.

I think I should take a close look at my insurance.

Good idea. The insurance aspect of our hypothetical hurricane is only one part of where we are going. A major problem that occurs after a hurricane is with looting of houses that owners left for safety reasons. Now suppose someone is arrested for looting and is held over for trial. Our philosophical discussion takes us into the areas of law and punishment. Criminal trials not only include physical evidence, they rely on the logical arguments presented by both the prosecution and the defense. The prosecution needs to establish guilt "beyond a reasonable doubt," a concept that does not have a direct quantifiable definition. On the other hand, the defense tries to argue that a "reasonable doubt" exists. The jurors need to individually decide which side presented the most compelling and logically strong argument. In other words, the amount of doubt that exists in the minds of the jurors.

So, if we look closely, trials often display philosophical elements of epistemology, logic, and of course science.

Yes. Now suppose a defendant is found guilty. This will connect other areas of philosophy, such as ethics and political philosophy because questions of possible punishment touch on questions of morality, law, and government. One of my teachers told a clever story that covers many things we are discussing. A person who was found guilty of a crime was given the opportunity to address the court before the judge pronounced the sentence. The person said, "Okay, I admit that I committed the crime. But your honor, my philosophy teacher in college explained to us the problem of free will versus determinism. Basically, it comes down to this: If we have free will, then we are responsible for our crimes, and punishment is justified. But since we are just part of the physical universe where everything is completely determined by physical laws, our acts are completely determined. Therefore, we are not responsible for our crimes, and punishment is not justified. I happen to think the arguments for determinism are correct. Therefore, judge, you should not punish me."

That's a clever argument.

116

Perhaps too clever. The judge smiled and nodded her head. She said, "You mentioned your college teacher. We might have taken the same course. I, too, was convinced by the argument for determinism, and I agree with you that I do not have free will. My sentence is that you shall spend ten years in prison with the possibility of parole. I did not choose to give you that sentence, my decision has been completely determined."

Hoist with his own petard. I love ironic stories.

Chapter 9

EXPLANATIONS

This provides the opportunity to connect our hypothetical hurricane case to the branch of philosophy called "metaphysics," the study of what are commonly known as the ultimate questions of reality. We just saw one example, the sentencing by the judge, which dealt with free will and determinism. Other metaphysical thinking deals with the nature of reality, the nature of consciousness, and whether God exists. That last one connects to our ongoing hypothetical case analysis. Imagine that after the hurricane devastation, someone who lost family members goes to their religious advisor for guidance and asks why it happened. Imagine further that the religious advisor gives a long explanation of the science behind hurricane formation.

That would be bizarre. I would be puzzled and upset with that answer. It's what I would expect from a meteorologist, not a religious advisor. I would expect some words of comfort, some reassurance and guidance about the meaning or purpose of the death. That's what I wanted when my younger sister passed away from a rare disease. For a while I was drifting, and my taste for life withered. Everything seemed senseless, fleeting, trivial, and there was no urgency to try to accomplish anything.

At times like that it is perfectly natural to question everything. The foundation of life seems to wobble. People ask whether life has any meaning. Is life and striving to exist at base an absurd proposition? Why would a benevolent and all-powerful God allow suffering and evil to exist? These are important questions that have been discussed for thousands of years and around which most religions have developed.

Recall that we used the term "Acts of God" to refer to natural disasters. It is a curious term when you consider the ramifications of how it is used. People often use other synonyms such as "God's will," to explain those events. But we should investigate what these terms actually explain. Compare the scientific and physical explanations of how a hurricane forms with the metaphysical explanation of saying that it was God's will.

Now that you put it that way, they are radically different. In fact, the metaphysical one doesn't really seem like an explanation

*at all. I guess it's just a placeholder word,
an admission of ignorance since we are
often told that we cannot know the mind of
God.*

Given a religious perspective, everything that
happens is an act of God. How could anything
happen "outside" of God? Here is something I find
strange: After some success, say scoring a
touchdown, why do some athletes find it necessary
to bless themselves and point to the sky?

*I imagine they are giving praise to God.
Their pointing to the sky is their
acknowledgement that the glory goes to
God.*

For letting them win? Causing them to win? Willing
them to win?

*I'm not sure how to answer that. I'd have to
think about all those choices and how they
differ.*

Fine. Let me add to the discussion. Are the athletes
giving glory to God, or can we instead interpret their
public display as a way of letting us know that God
gave glory to them?

*Perhaps it's simply an admission that their
success was God's will. That it couldn't
have happened unless God willed it.*

Fair enough. But that poses another problem. The athlete scores a touchdown and points skyward, acknowledging that it was because of God's will, or as it is often stated "by the grace of God." But suppose that as soon as that same athlete gets another chance to score a touchdown, he is tackled and breaks his leg. The athlete now seems to think differently; there is no public display of blessing and skyward pointing.

It would be odd to thank God for an accident such as that.

But that is where the inconsistency comes in. If we say that positive or good outcomes are God's will or God's grace, then why are negative or bad outcomes not God's will as well? When a winning quarterback says, "We won by the grace of God," he seems also to be implying that "The other team lost by the grace of God." We cannot limit God's grace or will to only one half of a sporting event. If winners win because of God's will, then losers lose because of . . . what? God's anger at the losing team? God teaching the losing team a lesson? God flipped a coin and we lost? It seems that once again we are told that in the case of the losing team we cannot know God's reasons.

Saying we can't know God's reasons seems part of what it means to be human, doesn't it?

But then why add anything to an outcome? If saying that we won by the grace of God is simply to admit that we do not really know why God let us win—or caused us to win, or willed us to win—and we do not really know why the other team lost, then why not remain silent? Why gesture or say something about God in either outcome?

> *Perhaps the gestures or words are meant only to give praise or glory to God.*

But how do we reconcile giving praise or glory to God for good results with the bad results? What words should we use to talk about God in those cases?

> *We say that the negative outcomes are a mystery because we don't know what God's long-term goals for us are.*

If the long-term goals are a mystery in the case of negative outcomes, then to be consistent, we should say the same for positive outcomes. If all outcomes are a mystery because of our mere mortal status, then a respectful silence seems more appropriate than unwarranted praise. After all, silence is the respected recognition of profound ignorance.

> *I will remain silent on that point. Oh, but I imagine that by my saying it out loud I violated my intent. Ironic.*

There is another curious point. Why would God expect praise? Does God have an ego that needs constant affirmation? We humans like to be praised and recognized for our deeds, but why would an all-powerful God need recognition? It seems like our praise is similar to those cultures who saw gods as powerful beings who needed to be placated by offerings, sacrifices, and prayers. What good are our offerings and sacrifices to God? And why would God need us to pray? Praying to God for something seems like begging. Making people beg for relief of suffering seems like a horrible characteristic for a supposedly benevolent God.

These mysteries are indeed puzzling. I guess it comes down to faith. And faith does require us to suppress many basic doubts. I'm probably getting stomach ulcers just thinking about this.

I hope not. Should we press on or change the subject?

No, no, please let's continue.

We can observe similar behavior at other times that is just as puzzling. For example, when a catastrophe such as an earthquake or tsunami occurs, it is common to hear people say, "Thank God more people were not killed." That always seemed like a strange thing to say. If a million people were killed, then why should we thank God for not letting two million die? What would be the point? If natural disasters are indeed acts of God, then surely God could have prevented them. Since nothing can occur outside of God, nothing can occur outside of God's will. Given this, how can we reconcile God being omniscient, omnipotent, and all-loving? Those three aspects seem like an inconsistent set.

What do you mean?

There are paradoxes that have been argued about when you consider the three characteristics mentioned. You might have heard some of them. For example, can God create a stone too heavy for God to lift? Can God change God's mind? That may seem like a strange way of putting it, but no stranger than when people give God a gender.

I may have heard things like that, but never thought much about it.

Some resolutions to the paradoxes require an adjustment to the set of characteristics in order to eliminate the paradox. Other answers suggest that the paradoxes show that God is subject to the laws of logic, that God cannot do what is logically impossible.

Can you expand on that?

I will try. Part of the historical debate over the paradoxes revolves around the various definitions of the term "omnipotence."

Various definitions? I thought it meant "all-powerful." What else could it mean?

One definition is "a being that has no limits," but this leads directly to contradictory results such as the "stone too heavy to lift" problem. We can look at two possible outcomes of the question whether God can create a stone too heavy for God to lift. On the one hand, suppose that God can create a stone too heavy for God to lift. In that case, God is not omnipotent. On the other hand, suppose that God cannot create a stone too heavy for God to lift. In that case, too, God is not omnipotent. In either case there is something that God cannot do, which seems to violate the definition of "omnipotence." As such, the "no limits" definition has been criticized and rejected by some theologians who acknowledge the contradictions and who want to avoid them.

In order to avoid the kinds of logical paradoxes associated with the idea of omnipotence, it has been proposed that God has the additional characteristic of being perfectly logical. In other words, if we assume that God's nature includes being logical, then no logical contradictions should follow. Therefore, we should amend the characteristics normally attributed to God as follows: omniscient, omnipotent, perfectly good, and perfectly logical.

I understand. The additional characteristic of being logical seems to help. But why do I

*have a feeling that it's still not enough. I'm
waiting for the other shoe to drop.*

Your apprehension is warranted. It turns out that if
being logical is included in the basic nature of God,
then it is still not enough to defuse certain paradoxes
that arise from the set of characteristics attributable
to God. For example, even adding the characteristic
of being logical to God's nature does is not sufficient
to explain why suffering exists. Contradictions that
arise between being omnipotent and perfectly good
still remain. Why would a perfectly good being that
is also omnipotent allow suffering to exist? It seems
to be a contradiction for a being to be all-powerful
and to be able to stop suffering, but who does not stop
it, and yet that being is perfectly good.

Other paradoxes arise between the natures
attributable to God. Being omniscient means God
knows everything. But can God change something
that God already willed? In simpler words, can God
change God's mind? Changing one's mind seems to
imply that some future that would have been is no
longer possible, or that God can go back and change
something that God already willed. But since
omniscience implies knowing everything that has
happened and will happen, how could any change
occur if everything is already known?

Returning once again to the question of why
suffering exists, it has been claimed that the total
amount of happiness outweighs the total amount of
suffering. I find that to be an absurd claim, not only
because it cannot be verified, but it also seems to

accept either the position that God willingly allows pain and suffering to occur even though God could easily prevent it, or the position that pain and suffering are not considered bad things to God. I find both those positions to be at odds with even the most basic human ideas regarding morally acceptable behavior, and they show the extraordinary lengths that people will go to hold on to beliefs that fail the touchstones of logic and credibility. We humans are subject to the demands of morality, but is God exempt? That same attitude of disregard for the touchstones of reason affords the same basis for fanaticism, despotism, superstition, and quackery of all kinds. It is a danger to humanity.

What about the argument that God allows suffering and evil because God gave humans the gift of free will, so life is a kind of probation. If so, then God does not interfere with our decisions because we must prove ourselves to be moral beings. In order to have any value, salvation has to be earned.

Then God places us in a position to make moral decisions that can result in pain in suffering, but God is off the hook? If I am in a position to stop pain and suffering but I fail to do so, then I am condemned as a bad person. But the same does not hold for God who can surely stop every instance of pain and suffering? That unfairness is at best an offense to our sense of morality, and at worst a grotesque indictment of God's "benevolence."

And that only takes into consideration actions of humans that result in pain and suffering. How does endowing us with free will absolve God of allowing natural disasters to occur that kill millions of people? The amount of pain and suffering that has occurred from natural disasters over time is staggering. Are we to believe that these instances are part of God's overall plan which we cannot understand? What are natural disasters other than the effects of God creating the world? Effects that are impossible for us to stop, but not impossible for an omniscient God who knows everything that will happen, and an omnipotent God who has the power to stop all suffering, and especially for a perfectly good being.

We run into difficulties when we apply terms that refer to physical processes to a metaphysical topic— God. The belief in a God is based mostly on feeling, not physical evidence. For the most part, we typically talk about earthquakes and tsunamis as physical processes. But some religious people claim that those things are the result of sinful behavior, so God is justified in causing the earthquakes or tsunamis as punishment. But can we rationally and morally accept that the death of millions of people, many of them innocent babies and children, is an acceptable response by God to sinful behavior?

Can you expand on what you said about the terms used in explaining physical and metaphysical processes?

128

Sure. We can look at how we use the term "cause." Through our scientific understanding of the world we talk about causes in many areas, for example in the cause of someone dying, or the cause of a fire. The term "cause" in these cases is limited to the physical world and our understanding of basic scientific principles. But when we try to apply the term to the metaphysical realm we distort the term's natural meaning and reference into a supernatural sense that is difficult to comprehend. In other words, the language of science deals with physical objects and cause-effect processes. But when we talk about morality and God, the scientific sense of our terms no longer fits. The idea that God causes things to happen in the physical world puts a strain on the term.

In addition, when religious beliefs are invoked we see a shift in our language. For example, when we explain the cause of a death we invoke objective criteria, that is, we rely on evidence that can be confirmed by others. But metaphysical talk typically resorts to subjective criteria, such as "feeling God's presence," or "hearing God talk to them," or having "out-of-body experiences" leading to overwhelming psychological states of "awe or rapture," culminating in an unshakable belief or faith in a subjective experience devoid of any objective reference. These kinds of states of belief are insulated from scientific investigation because the attempt to apply scientific concepts does not fit.

Given our discussion, I can see clearly how these questions differ so radically from the scientific and epistemological ones. They arise from different world perspectives.

It shows how philosophy touches all aspects of life. A simple example of a hurricane shined a spotlight on several areas that philosophers explore, and how going down one path leads to a different aspect of philosophy. It shows how questions of truth and knowledge are related, and that the important questions of life require a commitment to follow fearlessly wherever our reason takes us.

The philosophical commitment to follow reason can be seen in the ideas of some Greek philosophers, starting with Thales, who lived over 2500 years ago. These philosophers began to challenge the idea that the world was run by gods who used their powers in arbitrary, unknowable, and unpredictable ways. The philosophers rejected old myths and supernatural ideas; they argued that the world follows rational principles, what today we call "the laws of nature." They used the term "logos" to refer to this general idea, but the term also meant "word." Over time, however, some religions began to use the term "logos" to refer to a single God who embodies the rational principles used to create the world.

Wait, does that connect to the line in the Bible, "In the beginning was the Word"?

Yes, and that offers us a good starting place to discuss some possible implications of that line, and to expand our discussion. The meaning of that line has been the subject of debate for centuries. For example, some scholars argue that the line and those that follow refer to Jesus. Others argue that it refers to an uncreated creator. In any event, since they all agree that God is eternal and outside of time and space, the term "beginning" might also refer to the beginning of the physical universe. In this sense, God thought us into existence the way an author conjures up a world populated with characters. This opens up several avenues. One such avenue was proposed by the philosopher Robert Nozick, who wrote a short but influential article, called "Fiction," that fits into our discussion. When we sit down to write a fictional story, we are not always sure where the characters will go, or what they will say, or what they will think as the story progresses. In a fictional world, the characters exist in a different realm from the author, and what happens depends solely on the author's imagination. Many writers have said that after a while their characters seemed to take on a life of their own, which of course is impossible since everything that happens in the story comes from the author. Similarly, if we consider the idea that God is the author of everything that exists, then perhaps we can use the term "author" in a way that is quite natural to us. So, we can ask the following: Do the characters in a novel feel pain or anguish? Do they have internal thoughts?

*That's tricky. Since they are fictional
creations of the author, they don't exist the
way we do, so they can't experience real
pain or have real thoughts. All that is in the
mind of the author. And when we read the
fictional story, we imagine the characters in
those situations, but we don't think they
have real experiences the way we do.*

When an author describes the pain or anguish that a
character feels, the character does not actually feel
anything; instead we project feelings on the character
that are familiar to us. And we do this because we
believe that we are real physical creatures. And if a
fictional character says, "I really exist," or "I doubt
my existence," those thoughts are created by the
author, the character does not "have" those thoughts
they way we do.

So, if we are the creation of God, and if we cannot
exist outside God's mind—and even saying that God
has a mind like ours is perhaps going too far—then
we are like the characters and the worlds that we
create in our fiction. We would exist purely in God's
thoughts, in God's "words." Given this, what would
it mean to say that God created a physical world that
exists independently of God, and how could that
happen? And if we "really" feel pain, and since we
are part of God, then does God feel that pain, too?

But if we are not characters in a fictional story,
our finite existence is such that when we write a story
we often do not know where our creation will go until
we write it, and we can change our minds and rewrite

any part that we wish. But if we are God's creations in a fictional world, then when I say, "I exist," it is the same as when I create a character who says that. But since God is eternal, timeless, and all knowing, from God's perspective there cannot be any surprises in the story thought by God. Nothing that happens in our fictional lives can be unexpected to God.

But if we are characters in a story written by God, then our idea of God was written by God, it did not originate with us because we do not create our own ideas. And could there be layers of stories? I mean, can we be a story written by an author who is himself a character written by another author who created our author as a character who wrote us? Sorry, I don't know how to talk clearly about those possible layers.

It seems to lead to an infinite regress of authors with layers of fictional creations.

Can you explain that?

There is a story attributed to many writers that may help. A person once claimed that the world rested upon a giant turtle. When he was asked what the turtle rested upon, his response was "There are turtles all the way down." In our case, there are authors all the way down.

That's good. And this gives me a lot to think about. Oh, hold on. If I'm just a character in a fictional story, then I'll have to wait until my author decides to give me further thoughts on the subject.

In that case, we are at the mercy of our benevolent author—at least I hope our author is benevolent. When, or if, you and I are given those thoughts, then we will pick up the topic once again.

Chapter 10

TERMS

Now seems like a good time to ask you a different question about philosophy. Why does philosophy use such formidable terms?

That is a common complaint, but I am always puzzled by the question. The history of philosophy has allowed many diverse languages to contribute to its evolution, which encompasses the entire intellectual endeavor of human thought. But in many respects, philosophical terms are no more intimidating than those of other disciplines. I suspect it is not the terms that are frightening, but the ideas that are developed using those terms. It is true that philosophy does challenge us to think, or rethink, some of our basic beliefs, and that can be difficult for many people. It is also true that many people expect too much from philosophy. For example, a student of mine who took an introduction to ethics course was disappointed that he was not taught how to act in every kind of moral situation. I asked him if he had taken an introduction to psychology course, and when he said that he had, I asked if he felt qualified to be a practicing psychologist.

That's good. What did he say?

Of course, he said "no," but he also said that the ethics course was frustrating because it first explained a particular ethical theory, but then quickly showed problems with it. And then another ethical theory was presented, and soon after the problems with it were presented. The whole course was like that. He said that it never showed a theory that did not have problems. I asked him if his psychology course had talked about some early psychological theories of human behavior that had been rejected by modern psychologists. He grudgingly admitted that was the case, but quickly defended the experience as showing that psychology has grown better over time. I told him to go back to his teacher and ask whether the currently accepted theories will eventually be overthrown. To my surprise, one day he came to my office and said that his teacher agreed that everything we now accept in psychology will probably be rejected in the future, but that was true of all sciences. The student said that he was upset by this, so he asked his teacher, "Then why should we try to learn anything if it will turn out to be wrong?" His teacher responded by saying that this is what makes the search for knowledge so exciting. The student surprised me again by saying that he decided to minor in philosophy.

Did you see the student after that?

I did. And to show you how strange my conception of time is, I met him while walking around campus one day, and I remarked that he must be finishing up his bachelor's degree by now. He smiled and said that he already finished his PhD in neuroscience.

That's funny. Were you embarrassed?

I was a bit because he looked to be not much older than when we first met. But then, as I aged, I realized that it was getting harder and harder to discern the ages of much younger people. I joked to my colleagues that when I started teaching, the students looked like they could have been my younger siblings; then after a while they looked like they could have been my children; when they started looking like they could be my grandchildren, I knew it was time to retire.

I'll have to remember that as I get older and closer to retirement.

Where were we?

Weren't we talking about the intimidation factor of philosophical terms?

Oh, yes, now I remember. We talked about how the terms were first introduced by speakers of different languages   and   in   different   eras,   and   how philosophers like to keep alive the original terms in languages such as Greek and Latin, which can prove to be off-putting to many students. In this, philosophy is not alone. Every discipline uses terms that can appear to be intimidating. I think what happens is that once you decide on your major, then you are more likely not to balk at having to learn the terminology in your chosen discipline because you know the terms are crucial to your career, and you are likely to encounter them repeatedly in other related courses. But students also seem to think that terms from other disciplines are not so important, so they respond to them differently.

That makes sense. I know that I was less likely to be interested in learning what I thought were obscure terms outside my business courses, so I just memorized the terms and the definitions to pass the exams. And that led to my quickly forgetting them.

Science introduces some technical terms that often cannot be put into simple everyday language, but some scientists try. For example, Einstein was asked if he could explain the relativity of time in simple terms. Without hesitation, Einstein said that when you are listening to a boring person, a minute seems like an hour. But when you are listening to a fascinating person, an hour seems like a minute.

That is a great description of the relativity of time. I understand exactly what he meant.

Of course, it doesn't help me understand the technical aspects of his theories, but it gives me the sense that if I tried hard enough, then I could grasp more.

I agree. It sparks an immediate interest because it places things in everyday language. But philosophy not only introduces new terminology for students, it also requires a commitment to follow long trains of thought, and that is something that many people have not been trained to do. Philosophical terms, such as "metaphysics," "epistemology," and ontology," are no more strange-sounding and intimidating than some terms from economics, such as "arbitrage," "derivatives," "fungible," and "horizontal equity," terms that appeared strange to me upon first seeing them.

That's true. It's amazing how often interviews with economists or stock traders contain those terms, but usually the experts don't take the time to explain them. They just assume the terms are well-known, so why bother.

A funny thing occurs in philosophy classes when the topic turns to metaphysics. Some students get excited and ask whether we will be talking about psychic energy, auras, pyramid power, and healing crystals. Unfortunately, for many people the new age movement has transformed the term "metaphysics" into "mysticism." Upon hearing that we would not be discussing any of those things, some students promptly drop the course.

Were you disappointed, or insulted?

Disappointed, a bit; insulted, not at all. Perhaps they were equally disappointed to hear the origin of the term "metaphysics." Long after Aristotle lived, his writings were compiled into specific books based on related concepts, for example, Ethics and Rhetoric. Aristotle's books on natural philosophy were compiled into the book we call "Physics." The compilers then grouped together a number of writings and placed it after the physics book, and lo and behold, named it "Metaphysics," because the Greek word for "after" is "meta." The term has come to mean the topics that Aristotle discussed in the book by that name.

So, Aristotle didn't use that name?

No. But the name has become associated with the topics that Aristotle talked about, and in fact, they are topics that some consider to "go beyond" any direct knowledge of the physical world, so the word is appropriate in that sense, too.

Chapter 11

CHALLENGES

I must admit that I always avoided taking philosophy courses when I was in college. Maybe my being a business major had something to do with it, because at the time I just couldn't see how philosophy would help me in the business world. So I'm curious, why do so many people, like me, think that philosophy is useless, depressing, gloomy, and lacking in humor?

That seems to be a common belief. In fact, many of my students dreaded having to take an introductory philosophy or logic course. This attitude is partly a result of basic education practices, and partly because of the pervasiveness of religion. K-12 education starts out by teaching kids to behave in class and how to interact with other students and with teachers. Quickly, though, it inundates students with massive amounts of information that they are expected to digest and retain, especially through the high school years. The traditional means to check on students' progress is through standardized tests.

There is a lot of information that students have to know to function in a complex society, and we have gained a lot of knowledge about how the world works, so students should be exposed to a substantial body of important facts.

Facts are definitely important, but so is the ability to reason, and that is something we do not teach enough and where many students do not have adequate experience before they enter college. If you think about how different a philosophy course is from most other college courses, then you can see why students are afraid. Suddenly they are confronted with assignments that do not emphasize memorization or the parroting of facts. And for them, facts are what they have been exposed to, and memorization and regurgitation on exams is how they have been held accountable. I had many students who said, "I didn't know that you would expect us to think."

What an amazing statement. Nevertheless, I quite understand what they are saying. Philosophy does have that intimidating aspect to it.

As I said, it is simply because students are not prepared for it. But the emphasis on fact retention does not stop when they enter college because most of the courses will still be an extension of fact-based education.

142

But since they will need to be well-versed in whatever their major field has come to regard as the foundations of knowledge in that discipline, they are expected to have a certain body of knowledge.

No doubt. But the complaint made by many employers is that a lot of applicants with a bachelor's degree are not capable of working without constant supervision and hand-holding. They are not self-starters, they do not know how to critically analyze information in order to write proposals, and they lack basic logical and reasoning skills.

In other words, the skills that philosophy teaches.

Yes. You might be surprised to hear that many employers think highly of philosophy majors. Instead of being thought of as a "wasted major," enlightened employers know that philosophy majors can think critically, analyze information, and can write clear and precise reports. Those are the skills that philosophy majors acquire. And numerous studies have shown that philosophy majors' lifetime earnings eventually exceed most other majors and rival those of many science, technology, engineering, and math, the STEM majors.

That is surprising. Why isn't that more well known?

That is a good question. I think that even when the economic facts are laid out, many students still shy away from being philosophy majors precisely because of the factors I talked about earlier. It is almost as if they say to themselves that since my K-12 education did not prepare me for this way of thinking, it is too late for me to learn it in four years of college. Plus, having to admit to your friends and family that you are a philosophy major may be risking their wrath.

That's too bad, especially given the facts you mentioned about career earnings and what employers are looking for.

There are more surprising results. Many students who plan to become lawyers often major in political science, and students who want to be physicians usually major in biology or chemistry. However, students who majored in philosophy rank among the highest percentage of acceptance rates into law and medical schools.

Okay, now this is getting crazy. How can that be?

It is not that hard to understand once you know that law school applicants have to take the LSAT, the Law School Admission Test, and medical school applicants have to take the MCAT, the Medical College Admission Test. Parts of those tests are designed to assess logical reasoning, reading comprehension, written analysis, and problem solving, the skills that philosophy majors acquire in the course of attaining their degrees.

I didn't know that those tests were designed to assess those specific skills. But I guess it makes a lot of sense since a lawyer and a physician are both expected to apply reason and analysis to their jobs; they both need to be able to think quickly and clearly. I can see why philosophy majors do well on those tests, and their scores would probably be a major factor in their getting accepted into the programs. Nevertheless, I am still a bit stunned to see that philosophy is actually a great preparation for business, law, and medicine.

As I told my skeptical students, the studies and statistics are easily found online, so they did not have to take my word for it. But even knowing those facts do not, by itself, make philosophy any less scary for many students. I had many students who had specific topics that they feared. For example, I had students tell me that they would not do any assignments or exam questions that had to do with abortion or God.

Are you serious? They really said that to you?

Yes. As I mentioned before, the negative attitude toward philosophy is partly a result of basic education practices, which I already outlined, and partly because of the restrictive nature of most religions. Let me relate a story that illustrates what I mean. A friend of mine was preparing to get married in a Catholic church, and since a meeting with the priest was part of the required duties, he asked the priest if I could attend, even though it was supposed to be one-on-one.

Why did he want you to go along?

Several reasons. One, he grew up being afraid to talk to priests; two, he knew that I would not be intimidated; and three, he also knew that I would not say anything that would be embarrassing.

Was he right?

I will let you decide. The priest talked about the need to respect the ceremony, and the importance of recognizing that my friend was making a life-long commitment to uphold the marriage vows, both to the future partner and to the church. When the talk was winding down, my friend got a call about some matter that needed attending to, but I asked if I could stay and talk to the priest for a while.

Oh, no. I imagine that your friend was puzzled and maybe a bit afraid, although I'm not sure whether it was for you or the priest.

You might be right. The reason I wanted to stay was that I saw a book on the priest's table that I recognized. It was about a Pope who had died unexpectedly and the speculation that he had been poisoned because he posed a threat to the entrenched church hierarchy. I wanted to see what the priest had thought about the book. He was surprised that I knew the book, but he was also happy to talk about it. We had a lively discussion. I then asked him whether he planned to talk about the book to his parishioners. "No, no, no, I couldn't do that," he said, "They wouldn't understand. It would be too much for them." He smiled, we shook hands, and he said that he was grateful to find someone to talk to about the book, since none of his fellow priests were going to read it. I said that perhaps he did not give enough credit to his parishioners, that reading the book obviously did not cause him to abandon his faith. He said that part of him wanted to trust the people enough to talk to them about such books, and even to discuss philosophical questions about faith, belief, and God, in the way that he had experienced in the seminary. But he was constrained by the real possibility that some people would lose their faith, or perhaps report him to his superiors. I said that perhaps my recognition of the great gift of reason that we have compels me to follow it wherever it leads. He conjectured that perhaps faith does impose constraints on reason, but he honestly did not know whether that was bad or good.

Did you talk after that meeting?

He invited me to sit next to him during the wedding reception, but since we were not alone, we were not able to continue our talk.

I understand what you mean by the restrictive nature of religions. It is funny how the experts, the priests, rabbis, imams, and clergy, those who go through extensive training and who are exposed to speculative thinking, are reluctant to impart that thinking to their followers. So, I guess it's not surprising that many philosophy students are not prepared to engage in critical thinking and logical reasoning about religious topics, or even many moral issues.

Yes, it poses a serious challenge to philosophy instructors, a challenge that does not arise in most other academic disciplines. But sometimes there are revelations. For example, I recall one student who said in class, "It's about time that a course allows us to talk about the most important things in life."

That must have been gratifying to hear.

It was. I hope that some other students felt the same way, but maybe they were too shy to say it out loud.

Chapter 12

WAGERS

The unpredictability of life's twists and turns makes me wonder how mere mortals can ever make wise decisions. If sometimes we do manage to "get it right," then in many, if not most cases, it was a choice that we made without being able to calculate actual probabilities. Since in many everyday decision-making situations we cannot know even a fraction of the variables at play in the near and distant future, we cannot determine the probability that our decisions will turn out in our favor.

My penchant to view life as a constant gamble is perhaps an expansion of Pascal's "God Wager" to everything we do. In his famous book, *Pensées*— reflections—Pascal reveals his deepest thoughts about the important questions of life. For example, in his examination of the belief in God, Pascal recognizes that, at one point or another, doubt is quite normal. But he also stresses that we have a duty to try to overcome that doubt by concentrating on the ultimate end of life. For Pascal, if there really is a God who is omnipotent, omniscient, and perfectly good, then that being must be infinitely incomprehensible to us because our ability to reason about such immense powers is inadequate. But although our reasoning abilities are not up to the task of understanding God's powers, Pascal claims that reason does play an important part in the question of whether or not we should believe in God.

At this point in Pascal's argument it is necessary to know something about his accomplishments. Although Pascal died at age 39, he did remarkable work in the fields of mathematics, physics, and philosophy. His work with another famous mathematician, Pierre Fermat, on the foundations of probability theory originated in a gambling problem.

Was Pascal a gambler?

As far as I know he did not participate in games of chance. But he was asked by a friend to work out the details of some specific dice games. This was in the 1650's, so there were not yet any good mathematical tools for determining the payouts for interrupted games. For example, if for some reason a game cannot be finished, then how do we divide the game stakes, the pot of money wagered thus far, given the relative positions of the players? In other words, how do we calculate the probability of each player winning the game at the stopping point?

That does seem like a very complicated mathematical problem.

It is, and the solutions that Pascal and Fermat devised resulted in what today we call "expected value."

That's a term I'm quite familiar with from economics.

Their results were expanded to many fields by later thinkers. I suspect that Pascal used his work on gambling probabilities when he turned to his discussion about the belief in God. He devised a probabilistic argument to justify belief in God, which has come to be known as Pascal's Wager. The argument is quite simple. It is rational for us to believe in God because we can weigh two possible outcomes, namely what we gain or lose in wagering that God exists. Pascal asks us to consider these wagers. If you gain, you gain everything; but if you lose, you lose nothing. Wager, then, without hesitation that God exists.

It is a simple argument with important ramifications. A wager where we lose nothing if God doesn't exist, except that maybe we just went through life deluding ourselves hoping that we are right. It reminds me of the people who were rotten throughout their adult lives, and then at the end they repent and pray for God's forgiveness.

I find that attitude quite appalling; it is a last-second appeal to be pardoned for being a horrible person. I like how Pascal acknowledged that although trying to comprehend God's powers or trying to prove that

God exists is a fool's errand, nevertheless, he was still able to apply his probabilistic results from games of chance to his belief in God. Pascal argues that given our limited capacity for reasoning, we are inescapably tied to a game of chance. We are forced to wager either that God exists or that God does not exist. And for Pascal, everyone has to place a bet.

> *I like how Pascal married the idea of gambling to the belief in God. It makes a lot of sense, given that we are not endowed with God's absolute powers, so we are stuck with trying to deal with uncertainty at almost every step in our lives.*

But in most cases, unlike Pascal's God wager, we generally get immediate feedback from the empirical world. When we add in the biological drives that seem to make sense at certain instants, for example, when we say, "Why the hell shouldn't I do this?" which later turns out to be, "What the hell was I thinking?" It is no wonder we make choices that we later regret.

David Hume said that "Reason is the slave of the passions." In contemporary terms, this means that the evolutionary older unconscious parts of the brain, which are ruled by primal urges and drives, use the evolutionary newer part of our brain to achieve our primal desires.

I often have to catch myself when talking to my son. What might look like a suspect life decision on his part, at least to me, might actually work out for him. It is difficult to accept that he might be making the best decisions. I have to remind myself that he has far more information about his thoughts, his experiences, his desires, and how he sees his life and future, than I have access to. It is his gamble, after all.

Long ago, I thought about what Pascal and Fermat did, and envisioned a movie about their exploits. They were asked to work out probability calculations for various dice games in order to determine payout amounts so the game operator could be assured a profit. Paying out too much would result in the operator going bankrupt; paying out too little would result in gamblers losing too much too fast, resulting in lack of business. The time was ripe for the development of complex probability calculations, which Pascal and Fermat pioneered. There were some complicated dice games at the time, where as many as eight dice would be tossed at once, so precise probability calculations of all possible outcomes and various payout scenarios required strong mathematical skills.

I imagined Pascal and Fermat working out the probabilities for the various games, keeping the information to themselves, and then going around to dice parlors and cleaning up. Since no one other than Pascal and Fermat had accurate knowledge of the correct probabilities for each dice game and what the expected payouts should be, they would have a decided edge that they could exploit under the right circumstances. I think it would be fun to write the screenplay for a movie called *Blaise and Pierre*.

Toward the end of the movie, Pascal starts feeling guilty about taking peoples' money. He experiences strong psychological, moral, and religious internal dialogues as he wrestles with conflicting emotions. The result is Pascal's wager about God. In the end, the God Wager is Pascal's sneaky way of still continuing to gamble. So, how about this proposal? You write it and give me a fair percentage when you sign the movie contract.

That's a deal. Let's shake on it.

Chapter 13

PROBABILITIES

Although humans are confronted constantly with situations and decisions that require us to guess what will happen in the future, our innate skills are often not up to the task. In fact, we often make substantial mistakes in judging probabilities. Many of those errors come under the heading of "cognitive biases," unconscious reflex decisions that most likely have evolved over time because of natural selection. Decision making in a complex world requires accurate interpretation of relevant information, so getting clear on how, where, and why we use the term "probability" is quite helpful.

There are situations where we can say something is true or false regardless of our having any personal experience with the things involved. For example, we can say the statement, "All bachelors are unmarried males" is true by definition. Once you know the definition of bachelor it would be silly to do the following: You meet someone and say, "Are you a bachelor?" Now suppose that person answers, "Yes, I am." You then ask the person, "Are you married?"

That would be strange if you knew what the term meant. Oh, that reminds me of something that happened when I applied for life insurance. The agent asked me if I was married, so I told the agent my wife's name. After getting my wife's birthdate, the agent asked, "Is your wife married?" There was a slight pause, and then the agent laughed at his own silliness.

At least the insurance agent immediately recognized the absurdity of the question about your wife. The statement, "All bachelors are unmarried males," is referred to by philosophers as *a priori*, meaning the statement is true independently of any experience, other than learning the language involved. In contrast, the statement "It is sunny outside" is called *a posteriori*, meaning the truth or falsity of the statement can be known only by appealing to someone's experience of the weather outside.

Given a basic understanding of the difference between *a priori* and *a posteriori*, we can begin looking at some probability theories. The *a priori* theory of probability allows us to make precise calculations based on two assumptions: First, all possible outcomes of a given situation can be determined; second, each possible outcome has an equal probability of occurring. Consider a simple coin toss. How is it that we easily calculate the probability of the coin coming up heads? Well, since there are only two possible outcomes, heads or tails, each of these two possible outcomes has an equal probability of occurring.

So we are eliminating cases where the coin lands on its edge, and we are also assuming that the coin is not weighted unevenly.

Yes. When we apply *a priori* calculations we are considering an ideal world where physical factors are not at play. That makes the calculations straightforward. The probability is a fraction made by taking the number of positive outcomes as the numerator, and the number of all possible outcomes as the denominator. In the coin toss example, the probability of heads is $1/2$ because there is one positive outcome, in this case heads, and two possible outcomes, heads or tails.

A priori calculations can be readily applied to many games of chance when we can validate the two assumptions mentioned earlier, namely, when all possible outcomes of a given situation can be determined, and when each possible outcome has an equal chance of occurring. And that is why we can calculate the probabilities in coin tosses, dice, and lotteries. The assumption that each possible outcome has an equal chance of occurring is just another way of saying that the results are random.

This does not mean that any real coin toss, or lottery is perfectly random. It just means that we make our probability calculations based on the assumptions, in other words, in an ideal world.

Correct. We do not imagine that any physical game is perfectly random, but if we make a coin as equally weighted on both sides as is humanly possible, then after we throw the coin thousands of times we expect to see the results approaching 50-50 heads and tails. We can apply this same thinking to a toss of a six-sided die to calculate the probability of the number 3 coming up. Once again, our starting assumption is that each of the six sides of the die has an equal chance of coming up on any toss. The single positive outcome in this case is where the 3 comes up, and since there are six possible outcomes, the probability is 1/6. Using the basic principles it should be easy to calculate the probability that an odd number will come up on any toss of the die.

Let's see. Since there are three positive outcomes, 1, 3, and 5, and there are six sides, the probability of an odd number coming up is 3/6, or 50-50.

Right. Of course, there are games where the probability calculations are more difficult to compute, such as winning a lottery, but once you learn a few basic formulas, you can get good at it.

Another probability theory, called "relative frequency," relies heavily on our ability to observe and record the outcomes of certain events. These kinds of probability calculations are used by insurance companies. For example, the price you pay for car insurance has been worked out by looking at millions of people who were insured in the past. Car insurance prices are typically determined by factors such as age. Insurance companies have data about different age groups and the number of accidents and claims that each age group has shown over decades. Good empirical data are needed to determine how much they should charge each person, because the company has to charge enough to cover their potential claims and still make a profit, but not charge too much to scare away potential customers.

Relative frequency calculations are derived by dividing the number of positive cases by the total number of observed cases. For example, an insurance company has data showing the number of accidents and claims among those aged 16 to 21. These are the positive cases. The number of observed cases are the total number of drivers in that age group. The positive cases are the numerator, and the observed cases are the denominator, which allows the company to calculate the relative frequency of accidents and claims among that age group.

Yes, I am familiar with those ideas. If that age group has a lot of accidents and claims, then they are charged a higher premium than other age groups that have a smaller relative frequency of accidents.

That is why relative frequency is an *a posteriori* theory because it is based on historical data. But notice what the relative frequency is not claiming. The insurance company is not saying that a particular

16-year-old, say your nephew, has a specific chance of getting into an accident. Your nephew is simply one of the people in his age class, so we attach the probability to the entire class.

That makes sense. The company is not saying that he has, for example, a 65% chance of getting into an accident this year, they are simply saying that the frequency of the members of his age group getting into an accident is 65%.

Correct. There are other situations that fit neither into the principles of the *a priori* probability theory, nor the relative frequency theory. Professional sports gambling is one such place. Unlike most casino games which have calculable probabilities, the large number of variables that can affect the outcome of sporting events make accurate predictions unlikely. For example, the players that make up a football team change every year, often considerably. Players get older each year, they get injured, the players on the teams they face change, the weather, temperature, and field conditions under which the games are played vary from season to season. So, in order to calculate the probability that a team will win a particular game requires personal experience and a large body of historical data.

These kinds of situations use the "subjectivist theory of probability," in which we acknowledge that the calculations are based on a lack of total knowledge regarding an event. It is also called a "personalist" theory, but it should be emphasized that the subjectivist nature does not imply that the calculations are mere guesses. Another area where subjectivist ideas are used is in stock market investing; decisions are based on a combination of personal experience and the determination of what counts as relevant information for any given situation.

I am familiar with stock investments, and I agree that it fits under the subjectivist theory, and why making good investment decisions is so tricky. I know from personal experience that no matter how much I study a particular stock and the surrounding market trends, I still make decisions that turn out wrong. I see now that you used the subjectivist theory when you handicapped horse races.

Yes, but I was not familiar with that term at the time. When I did learn about the foundations and insights behind the different probability theories, I could see why gambling on horse racing was so difficult. Any decision or wagering that does not fall under the basic mathematical principles behind either an *a priori* or relative frequency theory of probability is going to have a huge uncertainty. The greater the uncertainty the greater the chance of losing.

Looking for patterns is a great survival ability that has evolved in many organisms, not just humans. Most animals will avoid a food source if they connect

161

it to getting sick. If you have a dog or cat who gets sick soon after eating the food you provide, it may take it several days for it to trust the food again. But although we have the ability to look for patterns, that ability is not perfect. While it is a good thing to be able to recognize a pattern that indicates a dangerous situation, we can overreact to certain sounds and sights; for example, becoming startled by a sudden loud noise, or reacting to a sudden movement that turns out to be harmless.

Looking for patterns is automatic and it occurs at any age. For example, I recall when my son asked me a question that caught me off guard. We used to watch old black and white movies quite a bit, so he was familiar with movies from different eras. We would also watch reruns of old TV programs, some in color and some in black and white. He liked to know the year that a movie or TV show was made, so I showed him that the date appeared at the end of most of them, often in Roman numerals. But since the date scrolled by quickly, he had to learn how to translate the numerals into the Hindu-Arabic numeral system that we use today. You have to be fast to translate MCMXXXVIII into 1938.

I always wondered why older movies used Roman numerals, and I agree that many times the movie goes by too fast foe me to translate the date.

I have noticed that many recent movies now use the Hindu-Arabic numerals. But it was a good way to get my son to learn another numeral system. It also allowed him to see why the modern numeral system is better suited for complex mathematics.

What do you mean?

There is a good reason why we do not use Roman numerals, except for when movies or TV programs were made, and for Super Bowls. Let me write something on a piece of paper. Okay, here it is. I want you to multiply MMCMLXXVII by MCMXLVIII. After you do that, then divide the first number by the second.

You mean without translating it into modern numerals? I couldn't do it.

I suspect most Romans had a difficult time, too. It requires numerous steps and is quite cumbersome, which is why modern notation is such a valuable tool.

And I see we got sidetracked again. Back to the story. By the time my son was around eight years old, he often asked how old I was when a certain black and white movie or TV program had been made. He kept asking me this for a while, and then one day he asked me what it was like when color came into the world. At first I thought that he meant when color film was invented. It turns out he had been thinking that up until a certain time the world was actually black and white, so that is what cameras captured. He had no idea there was black and white film and color film. He simply thought that all cameras capture the

163

world the way it really existed. So, it was natural for him to want to know what it was like for me to have lived through the transition from a black and white world to one full of color.

I can't imagine how fascinating and puzzling that must have been for him. What did you say?

I was amazed at his thought process, but at the same time I could see why the thought occurred to him. If you assume that cameras capture the world that we see, but you do not know that different kinds of film exist, then it follows that at some point color came into the world. When I told him the answer, he was a bit disappointed because he had wanted to know what it felt like to have gone through the transition. He still likes black and white movies because they are better at certain things; for example, the film noir movies that let the viewer focus on the people and the stark urban settings instead of being distracted by dazzling colors.

I never thought of that, but he's right. Black and white film is perfect for those old private eye movies.

Yes it is. And my son noticed something that I had not realized. Those old film noir movies are filled with people smoking cigarettes, and the cinematographers used backlighting to effectively highlight the smoke. As my son said, the smoke became another character in the movie.

He's right, and that's another thing I never really noticed. Your son is quite perceptive. I'll have to look more closely at the smoke the next time I watch one of those movies. It will give me a new way to appreciate an old movie.

Since we are capable of finding patterns, we do it all the time, but the ability is often lurking unconsciously. We rely on it to fill in missing information or when we try to interpret something we heard. We often mishear something but we might not know it because our mind quickly creates something that seems reasonable. This kind of mistake was given the name "mondegreen," by Sylvia Wright. The phenomenon occurs quite often when we mishear the lyrics of songs.

That happens to me a lot, especially with songs where the singer doesn't articulate the words clear enough for me to understand. I remember when I was young, I thought the line, "Oh, what fun it is to ride in a one horse open sleigh," in the song Jingle Bells, was actually, "Oh, what fun it is to ride in a one horse, soap, and sleigh." I had no idea why soap was there, but it seemed to make sense at the time.

That is a great example, and it shows just how common mondegreens can be. You must have laughed when you finally realized your mistake.

I did, but if I hadn't eventually seen the lyrics spelled out, I would no doubt still have thought the people had some soap on board the sleigh.

I am sure that there are many songs where if I looked up the lyrics I would be amazed. Although we consciously focus our attention when we are trying to solve a problem, we are also subject to other unconscious cognitive biases that surface without our being aware. And when this happens we can be tricked into thinking that our belief is correct, even in the face of contradictory evidence.

The term "apophenia" means a perceptual error, where we misinterpret a random sequence of events as meaningful. In other words, thinking that a pattern exists when it does not. This phenomenon is readily apparent in what is loosely termed as the "Gambler's fallacy," which is actually the name given to several related errors of judgment having to do with probabilities. An easy one to understand is when someone thinks that since tails came up four times in a row, heads now have a higher probability of coming up on the next coin toss. This misconception can have serious consequences. For example, a betting strategy that has been around for a few centuries is called the "Martingale system." It can be applied to many things, such as coin tosses, roulette tables, sports betting, and even the stock market, but it is quite simple to understand. For example, if you are at a roulette table you can pick either red or black and bet $1. If you win, you get $1 from the casino and you get to keep your $1 bet, so you wind up with $2. But suppose you lose. The Martingale system tells you to keep doubling your bet until you win. For example, suppose that you lose five times in a row. That means your bet started at $1, then went to $2, then $4, then $8, then you bet $16 on the fifth bet. Your next bet is $32. Now suppose you win the sixth bet. Does that show the system was good?

Why not? You bet $32 and you won, so you get $32 from the casino and you also get back your $32 bet, so you won $64. That's not bad.

You say you "won" $64. Did you really? Did you calculate how much you invested to get that $64?

No, but it should be easy to do. I just have to add everything I bet to get to that point. Let's see. $1 + $2 +$4, + $8 + $16 + $32. That equals—give me a second while I do the math—wait, that can't be right—$63?

That is exactly right. You spent $63 to win $1.

Wow, that's crazy. Imagine if I had lost ten times in a row and then won on the eleventh bet. Then I would be betting a huge amount

*of money just to win $1. It might run into
thousands of dollars bet to win one dollar.*

Right. And that assumes two things: First, that you
have thousands of dollars to bet, and second that you
do not reach the casino's bet limit.

What do you mean?

Most casinos have a maximum dollar amount that
they will let you bet on games, including roulette. So,
if you use the Martingale system and you reach the
maximum limit, then you can no longer double your
bet to get that elusive $1 profit.

That's lousy.

It may be lousy for the gambler, but wise for the
casino. Now suppose you are watching a roulette
table and keeping track of what came up. There may
come a time when three red numbers come up in a
row, followed by one black number, and then three
red numbers in a row again. Some gamblers will
think that a pattern has developed and bet black on
the next spin. If they win—and they have a 18/38, or
around a 47% chance of winning—recall the two
green numbers—then they will take that as evidence
of the pattern. But of course there is a 20/38 chance
that they will lose.

*If they lose, then that should tell them there
was no pattern.*

168

You would think so, but some people will still think there was a pattern but they did not recognize it sooner so they missed their opportunity. For example, they might think that once the three red numbers came up in a row, followed by one black number, and then when two red numbers came up they should have seen the pattern and bet red. That red happened to come up reinforces their mistaken belief.

There is a similar mistake in sports gambling. Bettors often look for trends, for example, when one team playing at home has a history of beating another team. The trend may persist for a long time, and if so, the bettors take that historical trend and project it into the future. But a historical trend regarding sports teams is not the same as a roulette table, or dice, or a coin toss. In those games of chance all the probabilities can be calculated precisely. The same cannot be said for sports teams which change not only from season to season, but from game to game because of injuries, players being traded, or game conditions, and other variables that I mentioned earlier.

I see what you mean by looking for patterns and misjudging reality. It makes a lot of sense and explains why we make so many mistakes.

But our ability to look for patterns also explains why we sometimes are good at understanding the world.

169

For example, it is a large part of why science has taught us so much about the world. And since we know that cognitive bias and apophenia exist, we have the means to minimize errors by learning some basic math, probability, statistical, and logical reasoning skills.

Many things interfere with our ability to reason and make informed judgments. Researchers have identified unconscious psychological impediments that can cause us to make bad decisions. These are the cognitive biases we have been talking about. The ability to make quick decisions can be a great survival skill, but it can also hinder us on those occasions when careful deliberation is required to render well-thought-out judgments and decisions. When we are confronted with a problem, or when we need to make a decision, we often rely on past experience to help guide us. Our experience of the world forms patterns of thought, called "heuristics," that we use to make decisions. The heuristics act as templates by recognizing that a current situation is similar to previous ones of which we are familiar. We then act on that similarity and judge that the outcome will conform to the historical pattern. But of course we know that a great deal of uncertainty exists in trying to predict the future, so the heuristic method does not guarantee success.

Some simple applications of heuristics can be seen when a car mechanic diagnoses your engine problem. When the mechanic relies on experience to narrow down the possible cause of your car trouble, she is drawing on the heuristic method. Similarly, physicians ask you a series of questions to determine the state of your health and to chart out treatment. We know that both a car mechanic's and a physician's judgment can be incorrect; nevertheless, the heuristic method is quite practical. In everyday life we rely on heuristics, but we call them "rules of thumb." The strengths of the heuristic method are the simplification of the current problem situation, and the short time needed to make a decision. The weaknesses are that the narrow focus and quick judgment can be negatively affected by cognitive biases. For example, two car mechanics or two physicians that differ in their experience, knowledge, and training, may draw on different heuristics to diagnose and solve a problem, resulting in different opinions as to what you should do.

Some of the earliest research into the area of cognitive bias explored peoples' judgments regarding probability. Evidence showed that most of us make simple unconscious mistakes that persist even when the world tells us that we are wrong. Here is a famous example: Suppose that a nail and a hammer together cost $1.10. And suppose that the hammer costs $1 more than the nail. Under the assumption that the information is accurate, how much does the nail cost?

It must cost ten cents. But I have a feeling that you are setting me up for a big fall.

The good news is that your answer falls in line with what most people say. The bad news is that your answer is incorrect. Along with most other people, your cognitive process relied on a fast assessment of the problem, most likely because it seemed so simple. You judged that the problem was simply the sum of two figures, ten cents and $1. This unconscious bias causes you to overlook a key piece of information that is necessary for a correct determination of the answer. See if you can work through the mistake. If, as you guessed, the nail costs ten cents, then according to the problem, the hammer would cost $1 more than the nail. How much would the hammer cost?

The hammer would cost $1.10. Oh, wait a minute, that can't be right because the total would be $1.20. Hold on, I think I got it. If the nail costs five cents, then the hammer is $1 more than the nail, so the hammer is $1.05. Those two figures add up to $1.10. I can't believe I messed up such a simple problem.

You are not alone. It illustrates how easy it is for us to make quick incorrect judgments unconsciously, when deliberation would get us the right answer. As soon as you thought about it a while, you corrected the mistake.

We can see cognitive biases regarding probability calculations crop up in all forms of gambling. For example, suppose you flipped a coin 10 times with these results: 7 heads, 3 tails (70% heads, 30% tails). Although most people accept that, in the long run, the ratio of heads to tails will approach 50-50, some people believe that in this example tails are "overdue" to come up. They seem to believe two things: (1) That in order to approach the 50/50 ratio, more tails than heads will have to come up on future tosses, and (2) There must be a greater chance, a higher probability, that tails will come up on the next coin toss. Both of those beliefs are unwarranted.

The key to understanding the cognitive bias effect is to analyze the phrase "in the long run." All we need to do is extend the initial 10 coin tosses we listed—7 heads, 3 tails, or 70% heads, 30% tails—to a much longer run. Suppose we toss the coin an additional 90 times, and in that run of coin tosses, heads and tails come up the same number of times, in other words, suppose each came up 45 times. We can add these results to the initial 10 tosses. We originally got 7 heads and 3 tails; next we got 45 heads and 45 tails; thus out of 100 tosses we got 52 heads and 48 tails. This means that of the 100 tosses, heads came up 52% and tails 48%. We went from 70% heads and 30% tails, the initial 10 tosses, to 52% heads and 48% tails, and this result happened when the next 90 tosses did not have any more tails than heads since they both came up 45 times. Therefore, the ratio of heads to tails is already approaching 50-50 without tails having to come up more than heads. This shows that the first belief—that more tails than heads need to come up in the future to ensure a 50-50 split—is incorrect. And the second belief—that there is a greater chance, a higher probability, that tails will come up on the next coin toss—is also incorrect.

We can see similar judgment errors at work in decisions that are based on a "positive expectation bias." For example, someone might believe that since a streak of what they call "bad luck" cannot possibly go on forever, "good luck" is "overdue." The next coin toss, the next turn of the cards, the next roll of the dice is bound to go my way because good and bad luck have to even out in the long run.

A lot of people, myself included, think that way, at least at some times in our lives. But can it go in the opposite direction? I mean don't we sometimes think that we are on a winning streak, so we bet more and more?

Absolutely. This phenomenon is referred to by gamblers as "riding a winning wave." They often raise their bets as the streak continues until the wave crashes. This shows the contradictory thinking that can go on in the gambler. First, they think that tails are more likely to come up because heads came up so many times—my bad luck will end—and second, heads already come up several times in a row, I will keep riding the wave—my good luck will continue.

I can see how these examples are reflections of some psychological dispositions that lead us to see the world in a certain way. Are there cognitive biases that aren't related to gambling?

Oh, lots of them. Although people have identified dozens and have given them names, some of them have not been adequately researched, so they may turn out to be inaccurate representations of our cognitive functioning. But one that makes a lot of sense and can be readily seen is called "confirmation bias," and it has to do with how we assess information.

Since most of us are inundated with information on a daily basis, and since unlimited information is just a click away, we need to filter much of it. But our filtering mechanisms often cause us to minimize the importance of evidence that goes against our beliefs, or even to reject out of hand evidence that challenges those beliefs. This affects what we look at, such as the news sources we rely on, and it often causes us to seek out information that merely reinforces our beliefs.

That explains why some people watch only certain news channels, or go back to the same websites over and over again.

It results in closing our mind, so our prejudices go unchallenged. For example, many experiments have shown that people provided with information that supports their belief about a topic are more likely to not only recall that evidence, but also to forget information that goes against their belief. This shows how we are unconsciously biased toward seeking out information that reaffirms our beliefs, and dismissing

175

negative evidence no matter how compelling it might be.

Would you care to try your hand at a puzzle that lends itself to some of what we have been talking about?

I'd love to. It will give me another chance to show off my weak analytical skills.

Not at all. But it will show how difficult it is for us to think about some things that seem so obvious, and how our cognitive filtering abilities sometimes let us down. If you recall, we defined a fair game, and the possibility of winning and losing strategies in certain games. Suppose you are chosen to play a game. The game show host shows you three doors. You are told that there is nothing behind two of the doors, but behind one door is a new car. The car has been placed randomly behind one of the doors. Although the game show host is told which door the car is behind, she has nothing to do with where it was placed. You are asked to pick one door. Here is a sketch of the situation:

| 1 | 2 | 3 |

Given this setup, what is the probability that the car is behind door #1?

That's easy. Since there are three doors, and the car is placed randomly behind one of them, the probably that it is behind door #1 is one out of three, or 1/3.

Correct. And the same holds for door #2 and door #3?

Yes.

So, whichever door you pick has a 1/3 chance of having the car behind it. We can add that to our sketch.

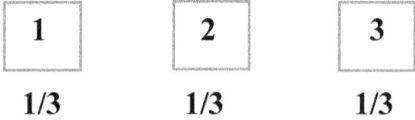

1/3   1/3   1/3

Is there a winning strategy in this game?

No, because whichever door I pick has only a 1/3 chance of having the car behind it, and that means there is a 2/3 chance of my pick being incorrect.

Great. We know that 2/3 of the time the car will be behind one of the two doors you did not pick. So, in this game there is no winning strategy. If we play the game over and over, in the long run you will win 1/3 of the time and lose 2/3 of the time.

I agree.

We can go ahead and play the game anyway. Which

door do you want?

I'll take door #2.

Any special reason?

No, it's as good as any, given the way the game has been designed.

Let me tell you a story. Over the years, I have presented this game to hundreds of classes. I had them vote on which door they wanted. Not once did the majority of a class vote for door #1. They always chose either door #2 or door #3, even though they agreed, like you, that each door has a 1/3 chance of having the car behind it.

That's funny.

I think it is quite fascinating because logically all the groups of students agreed that it does not matter which door they pick, but psychologically something always seemed to scare them away from picking door #1.

Now that I think about it, I also avoided picking door #1, but I can't really say why. Right before I made my choice, I knew logically that it didn't matter.

I was curious to see what you would pick. To continue: We agree that, as the game has been described, there is no winning strategy, so in the long run it does not matter which door you pick each time the game is played. But we can add a new twist to the game. Suppose that after you make your pick, the game show host does not open all the doors, but instead opens one of the doors that you did not pick, and shows you that nothing is behind it. In our case where you picked door #2, the host might show you that nothing is behind door #1 or #3 depending on the game. Can the host always do this?

> *Since I picked door #2, that means that either door #1 or door #3 is empty because there is only one car. And the game show host knows which doors are empty. Wait, it could be that both door #1 and #2 are empty since I might have picked the door that has the car.*

Right. So in any case the host can always reveal a door that has nothing behind it. It is important to remember that although the host knows where the car is, she does not manipulate where it is. She needs to know where the car is so she can always open an empty door.

> *Yes, I see that.*

After the host reveals the empty door, she then says that she is going to give you one more chance. You can either stick with the original door you chose, or you can switch your pick to the other unopened door. What should you do?

Let me think about it for a minute.

Sure. But to help you focus on some possibilities, suppose you are allowed to ask some friends for advice. One friend says, "You should switch your pick because that is a winning strategy." A second friend says, "You should stay with your original pick because that is a winning strategy." And a third friend says, "It doesn't matter what you do because now you have a 50-50 chance of getting the car." So, what do you think of those three pieces of advice?

My initial reaction is to doubt the first two suggestions because I can't see either one leading to a winning strategy. Am I right that we defined "winning strategy" as one where you will win more than 50% of the time?

Yes, that is correct.

Okay, then I agree with the third friend. Since one of the doors has been shown to be empty, that means there are only two doors left. It's now 50-50. It doesn't matter whether I stay with my original pick or switch to the remaining door.

We can unpack your reasoning. At the beginning of the game you agreed that each door has a 1/3 chance of having the car behind it, right?

Yes.

And instead of opening one door and showing nothing behind it, what if all the doors were opened at the same time?

You mean after I made my pick?

Yes.

> *In that case, I have a 1/3 chance of picking the door that has the car behind it.*

And that means there is a 2/3 chance of your pick being incorrect.

> *Yes, 2/3 of the time the car will be behind one of the two doors I didn't pick. But the new game you described seems different because one of the doors I didn't pick has been shown to be empty. Now my choice has been reduced to two doors, so I have a 50-50 chance of winning whether I stay with my original pick or switch to the other door.*

Let me ask you this. Suppose after you make your pick the host creates another new game. Instead of showing you that one of the doors was empty, what if she said, "I feel generous today. You picked door #2. I am willing to give you doors #1 and #3, if you give up door #2." What would you do?

So nothing has been revealed yet?

Nothing has been revealed. As soon as you pick door #2, you are given the chance to exchange it for both door #1 and door #3.

In that case, I would definitely make the exchange because I am giving up a 1/3 chance for a 2/3 chance. I mean I get two doors for the price of one.

And you would do this realizing that at least one of the two doors—either #1 or #3—is empty.

That's right. But I'm getting two chances instead of one.

You are indeed. So now we can go back to the game where the host opened up one of the doors and showed it was empty. You were given the chance to switch to the other door you did not pick, but you decided that it was now a 50-50 chance, so it did not matter whether you switched or stayed with your original pick.

Yes, but now I'm not too sure about that. I'm trying to reconcile two ideas. First, if all the doors were opened at the same time, I would win only 1/3 of the time. Second, after one of the doors is shown to be empty, I'm now saying that my original pick has a

50-50 chance of being right.

You think that those two ideas do not mesh?

I don't see how they both can be right, because it would mean that somehow my original pick can be right 50% of the time simply because one empty door has been opened.

Given what we said earlier, both ideas cannot be right. Think about it. If we open all the doors at once, then you will be right 1/3 of the time. But if the host opens up an empty door, then how can your original pick be right 50% of the time?

It can't be. Now it looks like I should switch, but something is keeping me from accepting that.

Here is another way to see the problem. Instead of a game with three doors we can play a game using a 52 card deck where you are to pick one card. Suppose the game show host designates the winning card as the ace of hearts. You pick one card out of the deck. What is the probability that you picked the ace of hearts?

Since there are 52 cards, my chance of picking the ace of hearts is 1/52.

And the chance of not picking it is 51/52, correct?

183

Yes.

Suppose you are holding the card you picked but you are not allowed to look at it. The host is holding the 51 cards you did not pick, and of course she is allowed to look at them. At this point, she looks at her cards and starts showing you, one at a time, cards you did not pick, and each time revealing a card that is not the ace of hearts. She does this over and over until she gets down to one card. You have the card you originally picked, and she has one card left. She now gives you the choice of keeping the card you picked or switching to the one card she is holding. What should you do?

> *I would switch! She had 51 cards and I had one, so of course she has a 51/52 chance of having the ace of hearts. If I get to play this game over and over, I would definitely switch each time because I would have a 51/52 chance of winning in the long run.*

And how about the three doors game?

> *It is based on the same principles as the deck of cards. I should switch doors each time.*

Is that a winning strategy?

> *Yes, I will win 2/3 of the time by switching.*

184

I'm amazed at how strong the psychological pull is to believe it is a 50-50 chance, and the negative affect on my ability to accept the mathematical and logical answer.

Chapter 14

UNPREDICTABILITIES

Unpredictability comes in several flavors. When I was part of a group of American university instructors hired to teach in Southeast Asia, we struggled going from driving on the right side of the road in the United States to learning how to drive on the left side, British-style. My colleague, Robert, bought a car with a manual shift. But since he was now sitting on the right side of the car, that meant having to shift gears with his left hand instead of his right. It was difficult for me, too. At first, my left hand would miss the stick, so I had to always look down at my hand and focus on its placement. The gas pedal, the brake and the clutch pedal were positioned the same as in the U.S., so that did not cause any problems.

Driving on the left side of the road presented several unique challenges, most of them perceptual. Driving for years in the U.S. trains your brain to look at the road and instantly judge your position, so eventually you can do a lot of things on muscle memory. For example, in the U.S., when you come to an intersection and need to make a right hand turn, you will wind up on the right side of the road you are entering, so it is an easy maneuver. But when driving British-style, if you want to make a right hand turn you have to steer the car into the left side of the road you are entering because you are driving on the left side of the road. But if you are making a left turn all you have to do is stay on the left side of the road you are entering. Those two movements are the opposite of what we do in the U.S., so it takes a long time to train the brain and muscles, and for some people it never becomes automatic.

It may not be obvious, but walking is also tricky. If you want to cross a street in the U.S., which way do you look before crossing?

> *You're supposed to look both ways, but my immediate reaction would be to look left because that's where the cars would be coming from as I stepped out.*

Yes, but the opposite is true for British-style driving. There you need to look right because that is where the cars are coming from as you step out.

> *I have seen many movies where people drive on the left side of the road, but I never considered how that would impact simply walking across the street. I'll have to remember that. It might save me a hospital visit.*

Robert lived about five miles from campus, and the hardest part for him was having to work his way through a roundabout. You probably have seen them. Most intersections in the U.S. have either red lights or stop signs. A roundabout is constructed so the traffic flows continuously, and it can consist of many intersecting roads. Imagine a large circle with six roads all meeting at the roundabout; that is what my friend was confronted with every day when he drove to school. Now add cars, trucks—lorries, in local parlance—buses, taxis, and motorcycles all converging on the circle. And the key feature of roundabouts is that the traffic does not have to stop, it can flow directly into the roundabout lanes. The particular roundabout Robert had to navigate had three internal lanes, the idea being that when you enter from the left lane of your road you should first merge into the outermost lane of the circle, and then work your way to the inner lanes depending on how long you expect to be in the circle. For instance, since there are six entrances and six exits to this particular circle, you may have to pass four exits until you reach your exit. The idea is to move to the inner lanes if your exit is not immediate. This allows the merging traffic to enter unobstructed. If you stay in the outer lane for the entire time you will hinder the merging traffic from entering smoothly.

Ideally, the traffic should be such that entering and leaving the circle is easy. In reality, it almost never happens that way. For example, quite often you will be in the outer lane anticipating your exit, but as you near your exit a vehicle may come barreling into the circle and intimidate you so that you quickly move to the next inner lane. This can be especially frightening when it is a large bus or lorry, and since the local drivers were aggressive, it was easy to be intimidated. And you cannot slow down because the vehicles are honking at you from behind, forcing you to either crash into something entering the roundabout, or to move over a lane and miss your exit. Since Robert was not aggressive, he often had to move over to the middle lane to avoid challenging an incoming vehicle. And to make matters worse, sometimes vehicles from the outer lane swerved into the middle lane, thereby pushing Robert into the innermost lane. At this point, getting back to the outer lane was an ordeal. Not only are you driving at a high speed just to keep up, you are constantly steering the car because you are going in a circle. Also, your perspective from the right side driver's seat is not as sharp as the one you were used to, so you can understand why he could not always get back into the outer lane in time for his next exit. He told me that sometimes he went round and round, so it would take him either 15 minutes or 45 minutes to get to campus. Unpredictability reared its ugly head when Robert drove.

Chapter 15

CONSISTENCIES

*I don't think I asked you this before, but can
a gambler win consistently?*

That is a difficult question to answer because there
are so many different ways to gamble. Suppose we
start with games that have straightforward
probabilities. Lotteries are probably the worst bet of
all. You have about a 1 in 7 million chance of hitting
the most common lotteries. It is more likely that you
will be struck by lightning in your lifetime than it is
for you to hit the lottery, even if you play it every
day. But, of course, if you win a big lottery payoff,
then you are technically a successful gambler. And a
few people have won more than one big payoff, but
generally that results from them spending a lot more
every week because they are multimillionaires.

The key word is "consistently." Can you win in the
short run? Yes. For example, you win a bet in roulette
where your payoff exceeds what you gambled up
until that point. Most people cannot quit while they
are ahead. And the longer you play a game that has
an unfair payout, the more likely you will leave

having lost money. So, in games of pure chance such as lotteries, to call a person who hit a jackpot a "successful gambler" is to stretch the normal meaning of the term. I prefer to limit the term "gambler" to a person who spends many years wagering on games that are not subject to pure chance and unfair odds.

I accept what you are saying about games of pure chance. But what about other gambling situations, such as horse racing?

Although chance plays a part, it is not a game of pure chance with precise probabilities attached to the outcomes, because a horse race is an event consisting of a huge complex of variables. In fact, all sports betting—football, basketball, baseball, hockey, soccer, boxing, and horse racing—comes under the heading of subjective probability. For example, a team's won/lost record, or a horse's racing history, is evaluated along with the present circumstances; for example, today's opponent in the case of a team, or today's race distance and opponents in the case of a horse.

Some people have compared sports gambling to the stock market since they both fall under subjective probabilities. Subjective probabilities have many more unknowns, or variables for which one cannot provide precise calculations, so they are not the same as simple frequency probabilities. The upshot is that the best sports gamblers and stock market investors look for small "inefficiencies" in the odds of an event. If you understand that *a priori* games have fixed probability outcomes—for example, coin tosses and dice—then it is easy to recognize unfair games that are stacked against you—casinos, lotteries—and avoid them like spam emails. On the other hand, if you recognize a game where you have a slight advantage, and the betting public is "on the wrong side of the bet," then the odds are on your side. Thus, being a successful gambler in these situations requires not only dedication, it also requires access to reliable data, deliberation, and determination. And even then success is not guaranteed.

Imagine an *a priori* game in which there are 6 yellow balls and 4 blue balls in a jar, and one will be picked at random. Suppose you are betting against someone who wants to bet blue all the time, and who lets you bet yellow all the time, but he is still willing to match you dollar-for-dollar. In this situation you cannot lose in the long run. You will win 60% of the time in the long run if you bet yellow every time.

Nobody would be that stupid to bet blue every time and still match you-dollar-for dollar. He will obviously lose in the long run.

Welcome to the wacky world of casinos and lotteries, where you can find millions of people willing to accept bad odds. When most people enter a casino or play the lottery, they know that the games are such that the odds of losing are greater than the odds of winning. But they are willing to bet anyway. Perhaps when it comes to casinos people are impressed by the setting or like the free drinks—as long as you continue to play—or look at it as a night out, similar to going to a movie or concert, so they are willing to lose a certain amount as an escape from their daily lives. The lure of lotteries is the possibility, however remote, of winning a life-changing event.

I can see how the psychological aspects in either case can override the logical and mathematical reasoning that is involved in accepting that you are making a wager with a low probability of you winning.

Now change the situation to a sports bet which is definitely not an event that has *a priori* probabilities because of the hundreds of variables involved. How can a gambler make a "wise" bet? By looking for inefficiencies in the odds. For example, during the 30 minutes or so between horse races, the odds of each horse in the upcoming race are determined by the amount of money the betting public has wagered on each horse in the race. These odds are continually updated every 30 seconds or so. Here is where all the subjective probability skills are applied. By calculating the subjective probability of each horse winning, you can compare that with how the public is betting. For example, suppose you calculate that the odds of the #2 horse winning should be 3-1. This is a subjective probability, based on the gambler's assessment of all the past and present information regarding each horse in the race—for example, the particular track, the race distance, the weight each horse is assigned to carry, the post position—the horse's position in the starting gate—the track conditions, each horse's recent workouts, the level of race—claiming, allowance, stakes—and various statistical information available, such as the jockey's and trainer's win percentages, return on investment, class drop, and many other variables.

That's a lot of information to digest.

It is, and that is a major reason why consistently picking winners in horse races is so difficult. Every gambler has to determine how much importance to give each piece of information.

That explains why the odds on each horse shifts over time as the bettors begin deciding which horse to bet on.

Correct. Now suppose the betting public sees the race differently than you. You gave the #2 horse 3-1 odds of winning, but imagine that the betting public has made the odds 6-1 on the #2 horse. That is double what you have calculated. Therefore, betting on the #2 horse is a "wise" bet, based on your subjective probability calculations. On the other hand, if the betting public has made the #2 horse 1-1, then you should avoid betting, since the odds are lower than you are willing to accept.

That sounds like something most people would not even think about, but it is a remarkably clear and useful way of thinking.

With the advent of powerful computers and sophisticated software developed by teams of gamblers with lots of money, those teams can do incredibly powerful calculations to exploit even the smallest inefficiencies that are in their favor. Are they guaranteed to win? No, of course not, since there are unforeseen, chance occurrences that cannot be calculated and can derail your chances of winning, such as the jockey falling off during the race, or your horse getting temporarily stuck in the gate, or your horse stumbling at the start, or your horse getting blocked in by other horses, or the jockey committing a foul and getting disqualified, to mention only a few of the things that can go wrong in a race.

There are a lot of ways to lose.

Yes, there are. It is a common saying among horse bettors that there are a million ways to lose a horserace, but only one way to win.

What is the one way?

When none of the million ways that can go wrong happen.

That's good. And it makes horse race betting a situation filled with pitfalls and unforeseen factors.

It does, and it highlights how the "wise guys" approach uncertainty. Since their betting strategies take advantage of small gaps or inefficiencies in the odds—recall the yellow/blue ball example—they bet only when the odds are in their favor. Anyway, that is how I approached horse racing, but in a simpler way, since I did not have the computing power to calculate tiny inefficiencies.

Chapter 16

FOOTRACES

For a simple thought-experiment, we can break down a fictional one mile distance for a horse running at a constant speed of 25 seconds for each quarter mile. Assuming this, the horse would complete the mile in 100 seconds, or one minute forty seconds, which can be written as 1:40.

Suppose we use our imagination to see how a race might unfold with three horses competing. Since horses generally run at different speeds, the horse that runs faster than the other two in the early part of our hypothetical race can be called the "frontrunner." The horse that starts slow in the early part of our race, but then speeds up in the later parts is called a "closer." The horse that runs the same pace throughout the race we will call the "stalker" because it is slower than the frontrunner, but faster than the closer.

Now imagine that the frontrunner runs the following quarter mile splits: 23, 24, 26, and 27 seconds. Since this horse ran fast for the first half mile, it will most likely get tired at the end, which accounts for the two slower final quarters. When we add the four split times we see that the frontrunner ran a mile in 1:40. On the other hand, suppose the closer runs the following quarter mile splits: 26, 26, 25, and 23 seconds. Since this horse ran slower for the first half mile, it was able to run faster at the end. But the time for the closer's mile is also 1:40. In contrast, suppose the stalker runs the following quarter mile splits: 25, 25, 25, and 25 seconds. Given this, the time for the stalker's mile is also 1:40. This hypothetical race would end in a tie between all three horses, or in race terminology a "triple dead heat."

> *I understand. In horse races and human foot races there are usually those who go out fast and slow down later, while others lag behind and then catch up at the end.*

That is right. The Greek philosopher, Zeno, argued that the result of our hypothetical race is logically impossible. The two slower horses can never catch the faster horse.

> *But reality shows us that Zeno was wrong.*

I do not know who said it first, but there is an often used phrase that goes like this: "Who are you going to believe, me or your lying eyes?"

> *I remember hearing that, but I don't recall if it was in a movie.*

I can imagine Zeno saying it to a disbeliever. Zeno attempted to show that our picture of reality was

198

mistaken. The problem has come to be known as "Zeno's paradox." In fact, Zeno created several similar paradoxes concerning distance and time, in order to argue that motion is impossible—that it is an illusion.

Motion sure seems to be a real part of reality, but I'd like to hear Zeno's argument.

It is not difficult to explain Zeno's reasoning, but it does challenge some basic assumptions we make. For simplicity, Zeno reduced a hypothetical race to two participants—Zeno suggested a 100-yard race between Achilles and a tortoise.

A complete mismatch. Achilles should dominate that race. Wait, wasn't that depicted in a cartoon where a rabbit is pitted against a turtle? And if I'm not mistaken, the turtle wins because the rabbit is so far ahead during the race that it takes a nap.

I recall that cartoon, but I am not sure if it was a Warner Brothers one with Bugs Bunny, or a Disney one. No matter, we can look it up some other time. Zeno does not need Achilles to go to sleep in order to illustrate his point that Achilles cannot win. In order to give the tortoise a chance, Zeno said that we should give the tortoise a head start, so let the tortoise start at the 40-yard mark of a 100-yard race. Given this, the tortoise needs to run only 60 yards while Achilles has to run the entire 100 yards.

That seems fair. But Achilles will win anyway.

It is quite normal to think that way. In order to make the mathematics easy, we can stipulate that Achilles runs twice as fast as the tortoise throughout the race.

Okay.

The first thing everyone would acknowledge is that in order for Achilles to catch and then pass the tortoise, Achilles must first get to the point where the tortoise began—the 40-yard mark.

Yes, of course.

When Achilles gets to the 40-yard mark, where would the tortoise be?

Since Achilles runs twice as fast as the tortoise, when Achilles has run 40 yards, the tortoise will have run 20 yards.

Yes. When Achilles gets to the 40-yard mark, the tortoise is at the 60-yard mark. Notice that we do not have to know how fast each participant runs; we need to know only that whatever speed the tortoise runs at, Achilles runs twice that speed. This way, we only need to concentrate on the distance covered for each over time.

That does make it easier.

It should also be agreed that no matter how fast Achilles runs it must take some time, however small, to run a given distance—Achilles cannot run a given distance instantaneously.

I agree.

When the race began, Achilles was 40 yards behind the tortoise. But when Achilles gets to the 40-yard mark, the point at which the tortoise started, Achilles is now only 20 yards behind the tortoise. But once again, Achilles must get to the 60-yard mark, where the tortoise now is, before he can pass the tortoise. And again, it must take some time—however short—for Achilles to run to the 60-yard mark. Of course, when Achilles gets to the 60-yard mark the tortoise has moved on to the 70-yard mark.

Achilles has run 20 yards, so the tortoise has run 10 yards. Achilles is quickly closing the gap because he is running twice as fast as the tortoise. Achilles started off being 40 yards behind, then he was 20 yards behind, and now he is only 10 yards behind the tortoise.

Correct. But when Achilles runs that 10 yards to get to the 70-yard mark, the tortoise has run 5 yards, so it is at the 75-yard mark. Zeno is beginning to tighten the noose around our necks. Do you see why?

> *I think so, but I don't like it. Since it has to take some time—no matter how short that time is—for Achilles to run any distance at all, the tortoise will always run half the distance that Achilles has run. If I understand basic mathematics, Achilles will keep cutting the distance in half between him and the tortoise. But because the series, 1/2, 1/4, 1/8, 1/16 . . . goes on to infinity, mathematically it seems that Achilles can never catch the tortoise. Although the math seems correct, something is wrong. Surely Achilles can catch and pass the tortoise.*

It is not called "Zeno's Paradox" for nothing. Zeno wrote a series of similar paradoxes over two thousand years ago that have stimulated mathematicians, philosophers, and physicists to write hundreds of books and articles offering solutions. If this topic interests you, then it is easy to find material written at any level of technical writing that you might wish to pursue.

Chapter 17

COMEDIANS

I think I asked you this before, but the Zeno paradox has made me think about it again. It almost seems that Zeno was part of a comedy team where he befuddled his partner, like in the Abbott and Costello routines where Abbot would fluster Costello with twisted logic. I am not threatened by Zeno's paradox. In fact, I find it fascinating, and in many ways humorous, in an ironic way. So, I have to ask you once again: Why do so many people think that philosophy is depressing, gloomy, and lacking in humor?

I had a student who said that normally she did not like going to her teacher's office hours. But she also said that every time she went to the philosophy department she observed people standing around laughing. It seemed as though the atmosphere in the philosophy department was lighter than in other disciplines. And the teachers seemed genuinely interested in talking about anything the students wanted to discuss, not just the course material. Most philosophers generally read a lot of things outside philosophy, so they can engage people from all walks of life.

Then why is most philosophical writing so devoid of humor?

Do you find the writings of many disciples chock full of humor?

No, not really; especially most academic textbooks, including the business books I had to read. I admit that the business books and articles were decidedly dry and simply something that I had to get through. My impression of philosophy books, however, is that they are frighteningly inaccessible. If only there was some humor to lighten it up a bit.

You have to admit that a lot of humor is not universal. Quite often it depends on your particular set of sensibilities.

I agree. There are a lot of things I find funny but my friends do not, and vice versa.

So, when many people read philosophy, they go into it already presupposing that it will be gloomy and depressing. They do not go into it looking for laughs.

Yes, I find myself thinking the same thing.

Now suppose you turn on the TV and see one of your favorite comedians being interviewed. The comedian is asked whether most people get his jokes, and he says the following: "Only one man ever understood me, and he didn't understand me."

That's funny.

I think so, too. You might be surprised to hear that it was not said by a comedian, but by the German philosopher, Georg Hegel, who was born in 1770. If you had read that in a philosophy book, then you probably would not have thought it to be funny.

Probably not. But maybe that's because by the time I got to it in the book, I would not be expecting to find anything humorous.

Yes, but what if you started the book by thinking that some of it is going to be the lead-in to humor that will eventually be revealed. And even some jokes by professional comedians require a long set-up, often with little or no payoff.

Are there more examples?

I like to think they can be found in almost every philosophical work, but I also admit that I find some philosophers to be funnier than others, just like comedians. Maybe the trick is to imagine your favorite comedian saying them, or maybe hearing them as part of a Monty Python sketch. Here are two more for your entertainment: "We learn from history that we do not learn from history." "Everyone is the other and no one is himself."

They are not hilarious, but given the right setting and mood, I can imagine laughing at them. They almost sound like Zen koans, those paradoxical statements that contain unsolvable riddles. Who said them?

The first one is by Hegel; the second is by Martin Heidegger.

Were they trying to be funny?

That is a good question. Maybe they were frustrated comedians, or maybe it is dry humor meant to cause a slight smile but not roll-in-the-aisles laughter. Of course, taking any quote out of context is perhaps not fair to the author, but my point is that even in context, a lot of philosophical writing can strike us as funny, if only in the sense that it can lead us to think differently, and perhaps ironically, about our own thoughts and beliefs. Irony often causes us to smile.

What you are saying is that the doom and gloom that many people expect when they begin to read philosophy prejudices their reading, so much so that they cannot enjoy it on any level.

I admit that much of philosophy is difficult to read for several reasons. Many philosophers write for other philosophers, so their writing presupposes a familiarity with the ideas. Philosophers often use terms that are not common outside philosophy, or they redefine a term for their own purposes. Philosophers often write after long contemplation, and many do not spell out all the steps in their thought's evolution. Translations pose other problems. Things that were written thousands of years ago in different cultures are difficult to translate into modern English. Even contemporary writing that is translated runs into problems, especially if the original author has a distinct style that is hard to capture in a translation. I recall a teacher talking about an important and influential book called *Critique of Pure Reason*, by the German philosopher, Immanuel Kant, who wrote in the late 1700s. The book cannot be read quickly; its ideas require a long digestion period. My teacher said that some people decided to test the authorship of Kant's book in the same way that people have tried to determine if Shakespeare's plays were written by Shakespeare.

What do you mean? Who else wrote them?

There is a long history of scholars debating whether the person whose name appears on the plays was the actual writer. Several other authors have been proposed to be the real author, such as Francis Bacon, Christopher Marlowe, Edward de Vere, the

17th earl of Oxford, Mary Sidney, the countess of Pembroke, and Emilia Bassano. There were even attempts to have a computer program decide the issue. Programs have been used to determine authorship by looking for stylistic "fingerprints," for example, phases, grammar, vocabulary, and sentence constructions that distinguish authors. The computer program did not provide a definitive answer to the question regarding Shakespeare, but the computer analysis about Kant's book was highly enlightening. The program determined that the book was written by at least eight different writers.

What? How could that be?

The good news is that we already knew for certain that Kant wrote the book. The funny news is that the analysis confirmed what those who could read the book in the original German already determined, which is that Kant was a terrible writer. Even in the original, it had been acknowledged that Kant did not have one style. His writing flowed like a raging river making navigation perilous. Couple that with the added layer of a translation into English, and you have a recipe for a daunting reading experience.

Are students in undergraduate philosophy courses required to read Kant?

Some instructors do assign short sections of the long book. My admiration goes out to the scholars who are able to devote decades to understanding the book and who are able to distill its ideas into manageable parts. It takes great fortitude and a profound philosophical sensibility to do that. And since Kant's thoughts continue to influence not only philosophers but mathematicians and physicists as well, it is gratifying that we have scholars capable of making such an important work available to as many people as possible.

So good luck finding any jokes or humor in Kant's book.

Perhaps humor is in the eye of the beholder. When you listen to a comedian, you know that a punchline is coming even though you most likely will not be able to figure out the ending. When it comes, you realize how clever the comedian was to have tricked you by the unexpected result. This also happens when you read a funny story. The effect happens instantly even though we know the comedian is leading us down a path that will suddenly make an unexpected turn. The result causes us to laugh because although we have been tricked by the result, we are not threatened by our lack of being able to anticipate the punch line.

Compare this to an experience where something important is on the line. For instance, suppose that you had a job interview that seemed to go extremely well, leading you to conclude that you will be hired. If you are instead told that you will not be hired, then you might naturally be upset. In both cases—the joke and the interview—an unexpected result occurred.

You laughed when you heard the punch line, and cried when you were rejected for the job.

Logical analysis of arguments and the reasoning process involved in solving complex problems lie somewhere between a joke and a failed job interview. Most examples in a logic textbook are neither funny nor somber. Therefore, when we work through a logical analysis of an argument we do not laugh or cry—we mostly feel relief that it is over.

There is a joke that all gamblers get. A man happened to be chosen as a contestant for a game show. If he answered six questions correctly, he would win $25,000. He was allowed to pick a topic, and to his surprise, one of the topics was horse racing, a game that he had been following and betting on for forty years. He correctly answered the first five questions. The game show host said, "Now, if you correctly answer the next question, you will win $25,000. Here is the question: Can you tell me who won the 1983 Kentucky Derby?" The contestant said, "No, but I can tell you who came in fifth."

I don't get it. Why would he know who came in fifth?

As I said, most hardcore gamblers get the joke immediately because they have been on the losing end of a bet numerous times. He remembered who came in fifth because that is who he bet on. Gambler's always remember their losing bets.

Oh, I get it now. He remembered who he bet on, which wasn't the winner of the race.

Yes, painful as it might be, lost bets are hard to forget. In fact, there is a special kind of lost bet, called a "bad beat," that occurs when a seemingly winning bet suddenly, unexpectedly, and cruelly turns into a losing bet. For example, your horse comes in first but is disqualified for an infraction such as bumping another horse.

Chapter 18

SEARCHES

The search for certainty in the midst of a life of uncertainty played a large part in human history. Those seeking to understand certainty forged the foundations of mathematics, geometry, and logic, while those interested in uncertainty led the way to science.

Humans evolved in an uncertain world where life is a constant struggle to survive. Language and the ability to communicate between members of a group helped the spread of practical inventions and tools designed to mitigate the amount of uncertainty in daily life. Science helps us by discovering regularities in nature, but regularities are not the certainties which thrive in the domains of mathematics, geometry, and logic. These fields of study contain certainties, but they come at a high cost, namely, they are not about the world in which we live. This is what Albert Einstein meant when he said, "As far as the laws of mathematics refer to reality, they are not certain; and as far as they are certain, they do not refer to reality."

I think I read that somewhere, but hearing it in the present context clarifies its meaning.

Understanding the difference between certainty and uncertainty underscores the role of philosophy in the human predicament. This is illustrated by the philosopher, Bertrand Russell, who said, "To teach how to live without certainty and yet without being paralyzed by hesitation is perhaps the chief thing that philosophy, in our age, can do for those who study it."

Can you give some concrete examples of the main differences between certainty and uncertainty?

Sure. We can first explore the certainty side through some simple logical examples. Suppose I say, "A bomoh is a painter," and then ask you whether my statement is true.

I can't say because I don't know what "bomoh" means.

I was hoping that was the case because it will add to the understanding of the principles that underlie my next example. Suppose I said, "A bomoh is a painter or a bomoh is a shaman." Could you tell me whether that statement is true?

No, I could not for the same reason.

The statement, "A bomoh is a painter or a bomoh is a shaman" is a compound statement consisting of two simple statements, one on each side of the word "or." We say that each of the simple statements has a truth value—true or false—and so does the compound statement.

If I an unable to decide whether the simple statements are really true or false, then I don't see how I could know whether the compound statement is really true or false.

You have struck gold with the word "really." The short answer is, "For what we are about to do, it does not matter whether you know what is really true or false." This is the key point about the logic behind the example. To see this more clearly, suppose we let X stand for the simple statement, "A bomoh is a painter," and Y stand for the simple statement, "A bomoh is a shaman." Now I ask you to suppose that the compound statement, "X or Y" is true. What can you tell me about the compound statement?

If it is true, then either X is true or Y is true. Can they both be true?

Sure. In fact, logic defines two uses of the term "or." When both X and Y can be true at the same time, then we call that "inclusive disjunction." For example, "Albany is the capital of New York or Carson City is the capital of Nevada," is a compound statement made up of two simple statements. In this example, since both can be true at the same time, we have an instance of inclusive disjunction. But the compound statement, "Today is Monday or today is Friday," is such that both simple statements cannot be true at the same time, so that is an example of an "exclusive disjunction." In symbolic logic, when we use letters to stand for the simple statements in a disjunction, we write it as "X or Y." We can then stipulate whether we are using inclusive or exclusive disjunction. For our example about the bomoh, we can stipulate that we are using inclusive disjunction. Given this, I can again ask you to suppose the compound statement, "X or Y" is true. What can you tell me about it?

Okay, that's helpful. If the compound statement is true, then upon our agreement that we are using inclusive disjunction, I can say that both X and Y can be true, but at least one of them must be true.

Great. We can now apply this to our original example. We know how to capture the logical meaning of the original compound statement as "X or Y." Now suppose I say, "A bomoh is not a painter," and ask you to assume that simple statement is true. Since we already translated the simple statement "A bomoh is a painter" as "X" we can translate the new statement as "Not X." We do this by extracting the word "not" from the statement and placing it in front of the original simple statement. This may seem strange, but I recall there was a time when people said things like, "He is a smart guy—not!"

I remember when people did that, too. It was a sarcastic way of indicating the opposite of what was said in front of the word "not."

The word "opposite" is right on the money. In logic, we say, if "X" is true, then "Not X" is false, and if "X" is false, then "Not X" is true.

I got it. This is not so bad.

I am happy to hear that. And the reason we are doing this will soon become clear. But at this point it should be easy to see the next step. Now I want you to suppose that the compound statement "X or Y" is true, and also suppose that "Not X" is true. Given this, what can you say about "Y"?

It must be true.

Why?

Because of our stipulations. If the statement, "X or Y" is true, then either X is true, or Y is true, or both are true, since we are using inclusive disjunction. But if the statement "Not X" is true, then X is false. Therefore, Y has to be true because we already said that "X or Y" is true.

216

Eliminating X as true means that Y has to be true.

Yes, and I like how you acknowledged a few things, namely, that you based your analysis on stipulations, and your use of the word "if." By doing this you provided a logical analysis, not a factual analysis. By eliminating the need to know what "bomoh" meant, the symbols allowed you to get at the logical heart of the matter.

I can see that now. If I stayed hung up on what a bomoh was, then I would have been stuck with trying to determine whether a statement was really true or false, instead of simply stipulating a few things to get at the logic. So that's what symbolic logic is all about?

That is one of its main points. Using letters to stand for statements in English, and stipulating how we will use certain logical apparatus, such as "or" and "not" to simplify the task of determining whether one statement follows from others. What you did in your analysis was construct a deductive analysis of an argument or inference. Of course, symbolic logic gets complex, but the reasoning process you displayed runs all through logic.

Since logic relies on stipulations and definitions, it is not all that different from most things we do.

Yes, and the idea goes back thousands of years. In fact, we can see this on display throughout Plato's writings where he has Socrates questioning people and asking them to define what they mean by "justice," "piety," "beauty," "reverence," "goodness," and many other terms. Socrates gets people to offer definitions and then he sees where those definitions lead, often resulting in contradictions. Bertrand Russell sums this up quite nicely: "Everything is vague to a degree you do not realize till you have tried to make it precise."

I would like to hear more about Socrates.

Perhaps we can return to Socrates at a later time.

Okay, that would be good. But I have a question. If we can stipulate anything, then how can we be sure that our stipulations can be trusted?

One answer was given by the philosopher Nelson Goodman, who said that rules and inferences are both justified "by being brought into agreement with each other. A rule is amended if it yields an inference we are unwilling to accept; an inference is rejected if it violates a rule we are unwilling to amend. The process of justification is the delicate one of making mutual adjustments between rules and accepted inferences; and in the agreement achieved lies the only justification needed for either."

So it is a back and forth progression where the parts act as checks and balances on each other. That sounds quite reasonable.

I think so, too. We saw that if "X or Y" is true, and "Not X" is true, then "Y" must be true. The first two statements are called "premises" and the last one is called the "conclusion." Together they form an argument. This argument is valid, meaning that if the premises are accepted as true, then the conclusion follows necessarily. This is an important step because we have discovered a special kind of certainty. A valid argument is one instance of a logical certainty. But notice the price we had to pay. We had to accept some stipulations and definitions, and we had to suppose "what if" the premises were true. Only after all that agreement were we allowed to correctly say that the conclusion must be true. The "must be true" cannot stand by itself; it only "follows from" our prior agreements, from the "what if" parts that we accepted as true.

The value of symbolic logic is that the symbols allow you to bypass thinking about the common meanings of certain words, phrases, and statements. And since meaning is often driven by context, experience, language acquisition, social forces, politics, peer groups, religion, culture, and emotions, the symbol "X" neutralizes the normal process of deliberation regarding the meaning of a term or phrase, or whether a statement is really true or false. This suspension of common meaning allows you to

219

focus squarely on what logically follows if you accept X. Your mind now focuses on the logical consequences of accepting X, not whether you believe X is true or false.

By training your mind to suspend judgment on a statement's actual truth or falsity, you eliminate knee-jerk reactions that rely on what you believe is true of the world. Your mind simply has to focus on an entirely different question: "What follows from X, if I assume X is true?" Symbolic logic lets you work through the logical structure of an argument without being distracted by prior opinions and beliefs about the world. If an argument is valid, it is not because of any prior beliefs you may have; it is valid for purely logical reasons. And if it is invalid, you make that determination by applying logical analysis. Once this process is completed, then you can replace the symbols with words and see that the common language argument must also be valid or invalid as well.

To paraphrase Einstein's quote: "As far as the laws of logic refer to reality, they are not certain; and as far as they are certain, they do not refer to reality."

I like the idea of clarifying the meaning of "logical certainty." Can we do the same for the term "uncertainty"?

We can get at it first by expanding what we have done. I want you to analyze the following argument. Premise 1: X or Y. Premise 2: X. Conclusion: Y.

Assuming inclusive disjunction, is it a valid argument?

Okay, let's see. Wait a minute, can you repeat the definition of a valid argument?

Sure. An argument is valid when, assuming the premises are true, the conclusion follows necessarily.

Okay, I got it. If premise 1 is assumed to be true, and if we are using inclusive disjunction, then I can say that both X and Y can be true, but at least one of them must be true. And if Premise 2 is assumed to be true, then X is true. But since I already accepted in Premise 1 that both X and Y can be true, then the conclusion could be true, too. So, it is valid.

Your analysis was perfect until the last step. The key is when you said, "then the conclusion could be true, too." What did you mean by the word "could"?

I meant that since we agreed that if premise 1 is assumed to be true, then both X and Y can be true, so given premise 2, Y could be true.

Could Y be false?

Let me start over. If premise 1 is true, then both X and Y can be true, but at least one of

221

them must be true. If premise 2 is true, then X is true, so that is enough to ensure that premise 1 is still true. But now Y can be true or false without affecting the truth of premise 1. So, maybe it is not valid because the conclusion doesn't follow necessarily. Is that right?

Your logical analysis is impeccable. Since you explained why the conclusion could be true or false when both premises are assumed to be true, you have uncovered an invalid argument. The great thing about this logical deductive analysis is that every argument is either valid or invalid. There are no semi-valid, or almost valid, or partly invalid deductive arguments.

Since there are only two possibilities, that simplifies how we can talk about deductive arguments.

It does. We can illustrate what we have done to capture these ideas. I will draw a line on a piece of paper, and annotate it with some of the terms we have been using.

Deductive Analysis of an Argument

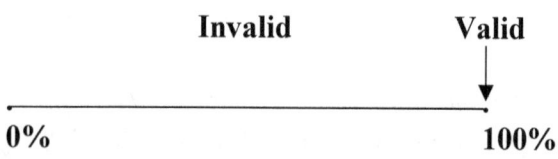

Deductive arguments are either valid or invalid. We can picture the relationship between the premises and conclusion by using a percentage scale. Since a valid argument is one in which the conclusion follows necessarily from premises that are assumed to be true, we can restate that as saying the truth of the premises guarantees the truth of the conclusion. The word "guarantees" is taken at face value, meaning that it is impossible for the conclusion to be false, if the premises are assumed to be true. The only place this can be on our line is at the 100% point because anything less than this does not fulfil the guarantee. And that means that anything less than the 100% guarantee results in an invalid argument. So, we can say for our purposes that a valid argument has allowed us to achieve certainty—a logical certainty.

I see why you specified that it is a logical certainty, not a factual certainty, and that's an important distinction. So, logic doesn't concern itself with factual questions, is that right?

The search for factual knowledge is outside the domain of logic, but logic does have a way to use the actual truth value of a statement, also referred to as the truth content of a statement. For example, logical analysis tells us whether an argument is valid, and if it is, then we can apply truth content analysis. If all the premises are actually true, then the argument is sound. But if any of the premises are false, then it is unsound, but it is still valid because the truth content of the premises is irrelevant to the logical analysis.

What if our logical analysis shows that an argument is valid, but the truth content analysis shows that while the premises are factually true, the conclusion is factually false.

That cannot happen. If an argument is valid, then under the assumption that the premises are true, it is impossible for the conclusion to be false; the conclusion follows necessarily. The logical analysis guarantees only what we will get under the assumption that the premises are true. This is a difficult idea to fully grasp, because it means that a valid argument may have factually false premises and still be valid. The guarantee regarding the conclusion is bound by the assumption that the premises are true. It makes no factual claim guarantees other than you can be certain that if the premises do turn out to be factually true, then the conclusion will also be true.

I see. It is easy to think that the logical guarantee says more than it does. The logical guarantee is specific. The drawing does capture everything we have been discussing.

The previous illustration showed us one kind of certainty, a valid argument, and one kind of uncertainty, an invalid argument, the terms we use when we do deductive analysis of an argument. But there are other kinds of uncertainty, one of which we are now in a position to discuss.

Inductive analysis of an argument differs considerably from deductive analysis. There are no different kinds of certainty or uncertainty in deductive analysis; arguments are either valid or invalid. But inductive analysis of an argument allows us to talk about degrees of uncertainty.

To help you better understand the discussion of inductive arguments, I'll add some new material to the previous illustration so you can see the difference between deductive and inductive analysis of an argument.

Deductive Analysis of an Argument

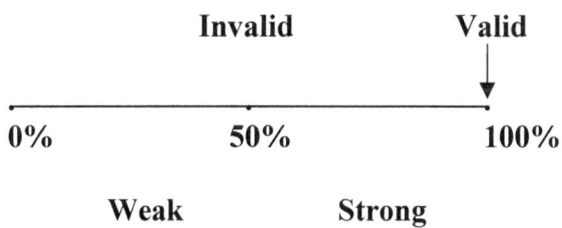

Inductive Analysis of an Argument

The inductive analysis is more complicated than the deductive, so it requires some fleshing out of the details. Notice that I added a 50% mark on the line. We did not need that for deductive analysis, but now we need it. The terms "Valid" and "Invalid" stay above the line because they are used correctly only when we do deductive analysis. The added terms "Strong" and "Weak" are terms that are used correctly only under the line.

We define a weak inductive argument such that if the premises are assumed to be true, then the conclusion is probably not true. We specify that as equal to or less than 50%, as indicated in the drawing. We define a strong argument such that if the premises are assumed to be true, then the conclusion is probably true. We specify that as greater than 50%, as indicated in the drawing. Notice that we are doing a logical analysis, not a factual one, just as we did for deductive analysis.

Why did you say that a weak inductive argument is "equal to or less than 50%"?

Because 50% is what we call a "coin toss," meaning in this case that it is equally likely for the conclusion to be true or false. Thus, we specify that a strong argument is one such that if the premises are assumed to be true, then the conclusion is probably true, in other words it is greater than 50%.

We also did truth content analysis for the deductive analysis. Can we do something similar for inductive analysis?

Yes we can. For example, logical analysis tells us whether an inductive argument is strong, and if it is, then we can apply truth content analysis. If all the premises are actually true, then the inductive argument is cogent. But if any of the premises are false, then it is uncogent, but it is still strong because once again the truth content of the premises is irrelevant to the logical analysis. The terms "sound" and "unsound" are used only on the deductive side, and the terms "cogent" and "uncogent" are used only on the inductive side.

I understand. It is important to keep the terminology clear and distinct.

You sound like René Descartes, the philosopher who famously said, "I think, therefore I am." He was fond of the phrase "clear and distinct." But we should not get distracted, so I will continue with the discussion of inductive analysis.

Since inductive analysis deals with uncertainty, the term "valid" does not apply. But inductive analysis allows for many more distinctions than deductive analysis. For example, suppose we have a box of 10 marbles in which 4 are yellow, 4 are blue, and 2 are green. Suppose that we randomly pick a marble, and you guess that it is yellow, but I guess that it is green. Our guesses can be seen as the conclusions of simple arguments. We are each assuming two premises as true. Premise 1: A box of 10 marbles has 4 yellow, 4 blue, and 2 green marbles. Premise 2: We randomly pick a marble. Your conclusion is the guess that it is yellow. What is the probability that your conclusion is true?

If we assume the premises are true, then I have a 4 in 10 chance of guessing correctly, or 40%.

Is your argument strong or weak?

Weak because the conclusion has less than a 50% chance of being true.

That is correct. And what is the probability that my conclusion is true?

Again, if we assume the premises are true, then you have a 2 in 10 chance of guessing correctly, or 20%. Since your argument is weak, too, that means they are the same.

This is where inductive analysis differs from deduction. Using inductive analysis we can say that although both our arguments are weak, your argument is stronger than mine. But we have to be careful. We are not saying that your argument is strong, we are simply saying that it is stronger than mine.

That's helpful. Whereas deductive analysis doesn't allow us to qualify any distinctions between two invalid arguments, inductive analysis gives us a way to qualify how weak or strong an argument is, and how it differs from other arguments.

Right. And it makes sense because whereas deductive analysis deals with certainty, which is all or nothing, inductive analysis deals with uncertainty, which is not all or nothing. We can be more or less uncertain, inductively speaking, but we cannot be more or less certain, deductively speaking.

There are other things that follow from what we have done. For example, if I say, "I will go to the party tonight," the truth value of my statement depends on whether I actually go or not, so we call this a "contingent" statement. In order for us to determine the actual truth or falsity of contingent statements we need to investigate the world.

So, if I say, "Mount Everest is the highest mountain on Earth," that is a contingent statement because we have to verify its truth or falsity by examining the world.

Right. The truth value of your statement cannot be determined simply by analyzing the statement itself. But now consider this scenario: Suppose you ask me if I am going to the party tonight, and I respond by saying, "Either I will go to the party tonight, or I will not go to the party tonight." Based on what we talked about before regarding disjunctions, what can you say about my compound statement? It might help to translate it using symbols.

If I let "X" stand for the simple statement, "I will go to the party tonight," then the simple statement "I will not go to the party tonight," is "Not X." The compound statement will then be "X or not X." Is that right?

Yes, the compound statement, "X or not X," is made up of the two simple statements. Please continue.

If "X" is true, then "not X" is false. And if "X" is false, then "not X" is true. So, one of them has to be true. But since this is a disjunction, the truth of either part makes the compound statement true. I don't see how the compound statement can be false. Am I off base?

On the contrary, your analysis was perfect. Based on your analysis, is this a contingent statement?

I don't think so. Since it has to be true, I don't have to investigate the world.

You are exactly right. And since you do not need to investigate the world, your analysis that the compound statement is true in all possible cases means that you have uncovered a logical truth, a "tautology" is what logicians call it.

If I want to make sure I don't say anything false, I can always use a tautology. That's great to know.

Be careful what you wish for. Think about what happened. When you asked me if I was going to the party tonight, I responded by saying, "Either I will go to the party tonight, or I will not go to the party tonight." But did my statement give you any information? Did you learn anything from my response?

I guess that before I asked you, I knew that you were either going to the party or you weren't going, so you didn't really answer my question.

Right. My answer, although logically true, provided no information about the world. Although tautologies are logically true, they are "empty truths," they don't teach us anything about the world. In contrast, because contingent statements can be either true or false, we learn something about the world through our investigations. That is how science progresses, not through creating tautologies, but by making specific conjectures, contingent statements about the world, which our research and experiments will eventually provide the necessary objective evidence that will teach us about the world.

This is another way to think about how logic and science differ. Science deals with uncertainty because they rely on contingent statements. But logic deals with certainty through valid arguments and tautologies, neither of which is about reality. Once

231

again, this helps to understand Einstein's quote.

There is one more thing that we can look at, if you are interested.

Sure. Please go ahead.

We can examine a statement that uses the word "and" in place of the word "or." The word "and" functions differently from "or" in that "or" allows three ways for a statement to be true. As we saw with inclusive disjunction, "X or Y" is true if "X" is true and "Y" is false, or if "Y" is true and "X" is false, or if both "X" and "Y" are true.

We call a statement that uses "and" a "conjunction," and it is different from a disjunction. In fact, the word "and" allows for only one way for a conjunction to be true, namely when the statements that make up the conjunction are both true at the same time. We can say that when my statement is a conjunction, the logical commitment behind my statement is such that I assert that both parts of the conjunction are true. This is quite different from when my statement is a disjunction, where the logical commitment behind my statement is such that I assert that at least one of the parts of the disjunction is true.

I think I understand what you mean by the logical commitment behind the statements and how they differ. Can we look at some examples?

232

If I say, "I am six feet tall," we know that it is a contingent statement that is either true or false. All you have to do is measure my height to determine its truth value. We also know that the statement, "I am six feet tall or I am not six feet tall," is a logical truth. But now consider the statement, "I am six feet tall and I am not six feet tall." What can you tell me about it?

Can I translate it using symbols?

Sure.

Okay. If I let "X" stand for "I am six feet tall," then "I am not six feet tall," will be "Not X." Given this , if "X" is true, then "Not X" is false. But since a conjunction requires both parts to be true, this means that the compound statement is false. On the other hand, if "X" is false, then "Not X" is true. But once again, this means that the compound statement is false. So there is no way for the compound statement to be true. I think that's right.

Yes, your analysis was perfect. What you have uncovered is the opposite of a tautology; a statement that cannot be true is called a "self-contradiction." It should be obvious why you should never contradict yourself, simply because your statement can never be true.

This applies directly to testimony taken under oath. When witnesses contradict themselves their statements nullify each other in the sense that their self-contradiction is logically false. In that case, their testimony should be considered inadmissible.

Since a tautology is an empty truth, perhaps we can say that a self-contradiction is an empty lie. One is trivially true, and the other is trivially false.

At first I thought that using symbols would be intimidating, but now I can see how it helps to separate the truth of statements from the logical questions, so my mind can concentrate on one task. Is that a technique that you used in your classes?

Yes. And as you said, it can seem intimidating, especially for students who disliked math. But once they worked with a few simple concepts, they became more comfortable with it. Also, students need feedback in the same way beginning driver's need feedback. The important thing is the feedback needs to occur quickly, so the beginner can make the necessary corrections. It would be unproductive for a driving instructor to wait a week before telling the beginner about all the mistakes that were made. The same holds for a logic or critical thinking class where instructors sometimes wait weeks until handing back homework. By then the class has moved on to new material, so the feedback is usually ineffective.

That makes sense. How did you handle that problem?

I had the class form small groups, no more than four in a group. I then assigned a specific exercise to each group and had them work on that exercise for several minutes, after which they presented their answer and analysis to the rest of the class. This served several purposes. It encouraged cooperation and discussion within the group, and the ability to communicate their analysis to the rest of the class. These are skills that students will need in their future careers.

I think that is a great idea. Instead of students struggling alone, each member of the group can help work through part of the problem. And bouncing ideas off each other is a great way to work efficiently.

That was the goal. It worked well. Students liked the idea of working together, and they made new friends, so that was a bonus. By the end of each class we were able to get through a lot of exercises, and the class benefited by seeing the correct answers right away. Plus, if the group's analysis or answers were incomplete or incorrect, it wasn't embarrassing the way a lone person might feel if put on the spot. The students welcomed the group interaction and they looked forward to doing the exercise sets.

Chapter 19

PROMISES

We are now in a position to expand on what was said earlier about how Socrates analyzed definitions of key concepts in order to achieve clarity, knowledge, and logical consistency. But since Socrates did not write anything, we have to rely on what others have to tell us. Plato's dialogues often have Socrates as the centerpiece of discussions, but at least some of what Plato wrote are his philosophical ideas presented through Socrates. For example, an important part of Plato's overall position is the realm of "Ideas," which are not physical things; they can be understood only through reason. They are also called "Forms," but since that term is generally thought of as something that can be visualized—a shape or a figure—Plato insists that the Ideas are not visualizable. For Plato, knowledge is attained only when we fully comprehend an Idea, so knowledge is conceptual, not perceptual. Knowledge is attained when we comprehend the essential characteristics of an Idea. For example, we draw an object and call it a triangle. Since a triangle is made of straight lines which are defined as having no thickness, what we draw is an image of the Idea "triangle." We cannot really draw a triangle because all our drawings will have lines with some thickness, however small. But through reason we can grasp the concept of "triangularity," a closed figure made of exactly three sides and exactly three angles, in which the sides are straight lines.

Grasping the essential characteristics of a concept is the true test of whether we understand a concept. For a challenge, we can explore the concept of a "promise." In doing so, we will need to formulate the essential characteristics that all promises must have. Our goal is to try to understand the concept of a promise in the way we understand "triangularity." We can start by creating a term for the Idea behind all promises, for example, the strange term "promisity," or perhaps "promisularity," or "promiseness" which sounds even stranger.

> *They do sound strange, but I guess I prefer "promisity."*

That would be my choice, too. In order to uncover the essential features of all promises, we can start by asking some general questions about promises. For example, why was the promise made, and who are the individuals involved? Suppose a parent asks a young child of, say, three years old to keep a promise about something. Can we expect the child to truly understand the motives of the parent? Is the parent trying to hide something that they perceive may be socially damaging, or perhaps not capable of being understood by the child? Or is it something that is potentially harmful or scandalous to another member

238

of the family? Is the child in a position to give an informed and rational decision, or is the superior position of the parent the driving force behind the child's acquiescence? What does a promise given in that instance have in common with a promise made between two equally positioned adults, each of whom enter the pact with eyes wide open and fully conscious and willing to enter the bargain? Further, when the child becomes an adult and can rationally assess the promise that was made, will that child be doing an injustice by revealing the secret behind the promise? What if the parent who initiated the promise is no longer living? Or what if another family member died, the one who was perceived to be in a socially compromised position? Does that promise still hold? Does it hold for all time? Do promises have no expiration date? And does the same hold for a promise made by two consenting adults? What points of intersection do these kinds of promises have in common, and by which we say that they both meet the criteria of the concept "promisity"?

Those are hard questions. Their complexity makes them difficult to unravel.

Yes, they are. And there are more. Are promises mere spoken words of agreement, or is there more to it? For example, suppose I teach my parrot to say, "I agree." I then ask if it promises not to eat for two days, and the parrot says, "I agree." Is this a real promise? Is it a real agreement? Or suppose I tape record my voice saying, "I promise." I then ask the machine to promise not to deteriorate over time, and when I play the tape I hear the phrase, "I agree." Is the machine agreeing to keep the promise? Does an agreement exist?

A promise seems to entail much more than mere agreement. Things like intention, rationality, and consciousness play a part. In fact, there are all kinds of agreements. Some can be classified as legal, such as a written agreement to pay someone for car repairs. Such an agreement is enforceable by law. Others, however, are classified as illegal, such as an agreement to kill someone, which is not enforceable by law. Promises can exist between individuals, between organizations, between states, and between countries. Do they all have something in common, and if so, what?

Suppose we conjecture that all promises have one essential ingredient: An agreement between rationally consenting parties. Does this single feature work? Does it make sense of the cases we talked about earlier, the ones involving children, and those involving consenting and informed adults? Or does it leave us scratching our heads because there is something that does not fit those cases. It may be that reducing all promises to one essential ingredient, say an agreement between rationally consenting parties, is too loose in that it includes cases that perhaps we do not want to fall under the concept, such as illegal activities, or perhaps it is too restrictive in that excludes cases that we might want to include.

It is not surprising that the usual examples of Platonic Ideas are geometrical figures because they can be comprehended through reason. After we experience many kinds of drawings of triangles we can begin to think about "triangularity." It is not that easy to have the same understanding of more complex concepts such as "promisity," or even one that we all seem to use without thinking much about it—"humanity."

That's a lot to digest.

Sorry, I promise not to do that again.

I won't hold you to that promise.

Spoken with true philosophical spirit.

Chapter 20

CHANCES

We talked a lot about probabilities, gambling, certainty, uncertainty, and chance. But since we are talking about concepts and definitions, do you mind if we discuss luck? I mean, what is it, and are some people just lucky and others unlucky?

Those are big questions, but we can give it a go if you wish. Although people use the term "luck" all the time, they probably do not have a secure foundation for what they mean, so they might be hard pressed to explain it or give a coherent definition. In order to get clear on some typical uses of the term, we can first compare it with other concepts. For example, can you tell me how you use the term "peer pressure."

I guess my use is similar to others. If I had to define it, I would say that it is a force that acts on people to get them to conform to some standard of behavior, such as wearing certain clothes, getting tattoos, smoking, drinking, drugs, or even religious beliefs and politics.

Can it act on any age group?

Sure, although I suspect we see its influence most often on teenagers. They seem to be subject to a lot of peer pressure, maybe because they are beginning to grow into adults, and they want to find an identity that makes them happy. But even older people are susceptible. Let's say a person spent his adult life in a northern city, and his job required him to dress conservatively. He might retire to south Florida and start wearing flowery shirts, Bermuda shorts and sandals because that's what everyone else wears.

That is a good example. I want to go back to something you said earlier, namely that peer pressure is a force. Can you explain what you mean by it being a force? I mean, the use of the word "pressure" seems to indicate it is something like atmospheric pressure, tire pressure, or blood pressure. Is that how you are using the term?

I guess so, although I never thought about it.

It might help if we see what is meant by some key terms. Pressure is simply a measure of how much force is acting upon a particular area. Atmospheric pressure is the force acting on the Earth's surface as gravity pulls the air to the surface. We did not have a good way of measuring it until the invention of the barometer. We also have a simple way to measure tire pressure, namely a tire pressure gauge. And we have blood pressure monitors.

The common denominator in these three instances of pressure is that we have objective measuring devices to accurately determine the force in each case. In all three cases we not only have concepts that we can define, we have instruments that detect real physical forces in the world. That brings us back to peer pressure. If it is a force like the three we have been talking about, then is there a peerometer that measures peer pressure?

Hah! I never heard of such a device. I think researchers use surveys or interviews to determine the extent of peer pressure.

That is my understanding, too. I think the surveys are also called "inventories." Researchers measure peer pressure by the responses given by the subjects studied. But notice how radically different this way of measuring peer pressure is from measuring the physical pressures that we talked about.

If someone changes her behavior, then do we simply say that the peer pressure must have been great enough to cause the change? But if she does not change her behavior, then do we then simply claim that the peer pressure must not have been enough to cause a change? Compare that with atmospheric pressure where we can predict and explain a storm. Can we invent a peerometer and take it around to a group of people to measure the amount of force exerted by the group? Imagine a researcher going around a classroom, peerometer in hand, and declaring that Room 128 contains twice the amount of peer pressure than Room 240.

> *That seems unlikely, outside of a science-fiction story. Then maybe peer pressure is not a force that can be measured outside of us, but only inside us.*

Perhaps, but then it should be like blood pressure which we can objectively measure. But I never heard of either an external or an internal peerometer. So, we are left with a person's feelings about how much pressure they felt in a given situation. If so, then perhaps the use of the term "pressure" is the result of social scientists wanting to make their conjectures sound like those of the natural sciences such as physics and chemistry.

> *But the natural sciences have a much longer history than the social sciences, so maybe it will take a while for them to catch up.*

Perhaps. But I seem to have taken us off course once again. I wanted to use the discussion as a way to talk about luck, so we can now pivot back in that direction. The question before us is the status of the term "luck." Can you tell me how you use that word?

Now that we talked about peer pressure, I have to rethink my position. I guess I see luck as something that pervades the universe and impacts our experiences. I mean, I think there are lucky and unlucky people. But, based on our previous discussion, I'm reluctant to say that luck is a force that can be objectively measured. Maybe all we can do is to observe the effects of it on humans, whether good or bad things happen to them, how often they happen, and under what circumstances.

That is a fine start. It gives us a framework for discussion. Let me run something by you. A lot of people smoke cigarettes, and a lot of people play the lottery. On the one hand, many smokers believe that they will not get lung cancer, but they also believe that they might hit the lottery. In fact, the odds are about the same for either outcome. If they get lung cancer, then it was simply "bad luck." Therefore, it must have been "good luck" if they did not get lung cancer. And if they hit the lottery, then it was "good luck." Therefore, it must have been "bad luck" if they did not hit it. In other words, "good luck" in the lottery means winning it, while "good luck" in the lung cancer case is not getting it. But since the odds are the same in both cases, they are hoping to "win" in one case and hoping to "lose" in the other.

They are taking a chance at two games, one where they might get lung cancer, and the other where they might win the lottery. But although the odds are the same, the possible effects of winning and losing on their lives are radically different. It seems quite irrational when we put it that way.

What it does is reduce "good luck" to a positive outcome in one game—hitting the lottery—but a negative outcome in the other game—not getting lung cancer. But it also reduces "bad luck" to a negative outcome in one game—not winning the lottery—and a positive outcome in the other game—getting lung cancer.

That sounds weird, but it also makes sense. We are strange creatures aren't we?

Indeed. Thousands of years ago some philosophers tried to explain what happens in nature without invoking supernatural forces. They wanted to explain earthquakes, hurricanes, and diseases as caused by mixtures and interactions of, for example, earth, air, fire, and water. Although we might say that is overly simplistic, the idea behind it was to eliminate the need to invoke such things as the mountain god who causes volcanoes, or the rain god who punishes us with too much or not enough rain, and who we must placate by offering sacrifices and prayers. Superstitions do not offer a way forward because they offer no mechanism for understanding the true nature of why things happen. Their only refuge is to stick our heads in the sand and wait for better days. Raymond Smullyan, who was a philosopher, logician, mathematician, musician, and magician, once said, "Superstition brings bad luck." And when asked why he was not superstitions, Smullyan said, "Because I'm a Pisces."

He sounds like a fascinating character. Did he really do all those things that you mentioned?

He did. He excelled at all that I mentioned. He earned a living for a while as a professional magician, and if he did not suffer from tendonitis, he might have been a great pianist. Raymond wrote many books on logic and mathematics, and many of his philosophical books are quite accessible. He also wrote some unique chess puzzle books. I highly recommend looking into his body of work.

Well, we have to get back to the topic at hand. Science looks directly at nature as the source of change, and it offers the possibility of either controlling some of the forces, or manipulating the physical environment, or at least anticipating what might happen so we can protect ourselves. Scientists talk about chance instead of luck. Chance is part of a complex universe that is, for us, fundamentally unpredictable. But chance is not personal. We tend to think of luck as a personal thing, where those with bad luck think the universe is out to get them. This idea can be seen in the following story. A person lived a life of utter torment. His family died under horrible circumstances; his career was dashed just when it seemed to get started; a flood destroyed his home. One day he could not take it anymore, so he fell on his knees and shouted to the sky, "God, why have you done this to me?" The clouds parted and he heard a voice say, "You know Tim, there's just something about you that ticks me off."

That's how a lot of people look at life. Either there is a god that hates us, or this awful force called "bad luck" follows some of us around waiting for the best time to defeat us. But if that's the case, then there must be either a god that loves certain people but not others, or the wonderful force called "good luck" follows some of us around waiting for the best time to reward us.

The term "chance" is often used in place of the term "probability," which sounds more technical. In a fair coin toss you have a 50-50 chance of correctly predicting what will turn up. We already know the probability of your winning or losing, so there is no mystery. But when we introduce "luck" as a component into the coin toss, it is used as a way to make the outcome a function of a mysterious force over which we have no control. We also use luck to rationalize what happens to us. Bad luck absolves us of being responsible for unwanted outcomes—the

249

world is against us. Good luck is a reward. But why should the world reward us for guessing heads instead of tails?

Perhaps we invoke luck simply because reducing outcomes to sheer probabilities makes the world too impersonal. Maybe we need the mystery to make sense of what happens.

It may be that understanding probabilities takes some of the mystery out of life, but science and mathematical applications have made day-to-day life more predictable and safe. It seems that when we use the term "luck" we are just referring to our internal response to what happens to us. Let me get at that point by using some results from the history of science. For a long time scientists conjectured that something called "aether" pervaded the universe. It was believed to be an invisible material, and part of why it was needed was to explain the transmission of light through space. Since it was believed that light could not travel through a vacuum, the space between the Sun and the Earth had to be saturated with aether to ensure the light got to us. It took many years of debates and experiments to overthrow the aether theory. You might not have heard of it because science textbooks generally do not spend time discussing ideas that were shown to be false. We now know that light can propagate through space, it does not need a medium like aether to carry it.

When was the theory first proposed, and when was it abandoned?

The idea was conceived several centuries ago, but the debate reached its peak in the late 19th century. The fancy name was "luminiferous aether," but fancy did not save the day. I offer this as an example of the concept called "reification." Simply put, to reify is to believe that an abstract concept has a physical reality. Reification happens all the time, for example when we trick children into believing that Santa Claus exists.

That reminds me of a friend who was so upset when he found out that Santa didn't exist that he planned to become a lawyer so he could sue his parents over the deception. He did become a lawyer, but I guess he eventually forgave his parents. At least I hope so.

That one deception motivated his career choice, and it shows the power of reification. Have you heard of phrenology?

No, what is it?

It was a theory that claimed the irregular bumps and slight indentations on our skulls are correlated with certain personality traits. Practitioners believed that certain areas of the brain control different bodily functions, which itself is not completely wrong. But the reason we now consider phrenology to be a pseudoscience is that the specific mapping of the skull that was developed proved to be too crude. For example, it was believed that all murderers have a specific set of bumps and indentations. If that is true, we should be able to predict who will be dangerous, and then use that as justification to institutionalize them to protect society.

Ideas like that seem to be fodder for science-fiction stories. I recall a story that talked about what we should do if we can predict dangerous behavior. In fact, now that I think about it, isn't this the basis for genetic manipulation, not necessarily for potential criminal behavior, but for the elimination of genes that will lead to debilitative diseases?

Yes. Although phrenology was a crude attempt to understand personality traits, genetic research and brain studies are similar attempts to try to predict the future. So, we can say that phrenologists reified their concepts. I have one more example of reification, if you care to hear it?

Sure, please proceed.

When we burn something, say a piece of wood, we notice many things, such as the flames, the heat, perhaps smoke, and the leftover ash. To explain how combustion worked, a 17th century idea was developed that was called "phlogiston theory." The theory conjectured that all material that can burn contains the element phlogiston which gets released during the combustion process. If we watch something burn, we notice that eventually the burning stops. At that point, so said the theory, all the phlogiston has been released, so there is nothing left to burn. It sounds convincing, but have you ever heard of phlogiston?

No, I haven't. I guess you're going to tell me the theory was abandoned.

No surprise there. Its demise occurred soon after the 18th century chemist, Antoine Lavoisier, devised experiments that led to the discovery of oxygen. So, instead of phlogiston being released during combustion, Lavoisier showed that oxygen was a part of the air that contributed to the burning. The invisible phlogiston was soon recognized as a fiction, another reified concept that had no physical existence.

So the history of science is full of ideas that were reified, just like superstitions.

Yes, but the difference is that science accepts objective evidence developed through rigorous experiments that must be replicable. People who believe in superstitions insulate their beliefs from any rational and objective assessment of the evidence. The insulation is the act of reification.

I see. Superstitions can embed themselves
deep into our behaviors.

Since the true believers shield their ideas from criticism, it is not surprising that the ideas last so long. And that brings us back to luck. "I was lucky," is a non-religious way of saying that the universe favored me for some unknown reason. It substitutes a force that pervades the universe and behaves in strange and unpredictable ways for a God who watches everything but who also behaves in strange and unpredictable ways. I see luck as one of the more lasting superstitions, so much so that nearly everyone uses the term. There is no real problem when it is used as an alternative to the term "chance," which itself is just a more colloquial term than "probability." The problem is that the movement from probability to chance to luck is a movement from an understanding of the nature of physical reality to a mystical belief.

Chapter 21

MINDS

An awareness of uncertainty results in some level of doubt in everyone. The level of doubt varies, from mild irritation to deep anxiety. When doubt infiltrates our consciousness it can be a source of motivation, or it can hinder our ability to act. Doubt creeps into our relationships, our job security, our health, how we view our government's policies, and even in the question of whether life is worth living. On that last question, I recall a teacher countering it by asking, "Is death worth dying?"

I see the point. In fact, I have often experienced religious doubt. It is something that creeps up on me, and it can be quite difficult to get it out of my mind.

Religious doubt may be the most difficult for most people to grapple with because it forms such a large part of our upbringing, and a major part of our personal identity. Doubt enters into both physical and metaphysical questions. Let me ask you if you think it is possible to doubt every belief that you have?

Every belief? I don't know. Where would that leave me? What could I hold on to for support? Is it possible to have even a single coherent thought if I doubted everything, including my understanding of language?

Good point. It seems that to have doubts requires a grasp of language sufficient and stable enough in which the doubt can be expressed. Our senses provide information of an outside world, and language gives us the means to talk about that world. But we also know that our senses are limited, and are often subject to how we feel. For example, your favorite drink may taste awful if you are sick. Since the world of appearance, given through sensations, is always changing, it is not surprising that our claims about what is outside us are subject to doubt.

The combination of language and sensations can lead to knowledge or doubt, two sides of a coin. Philosophers who hold that knowledge can be gained through reason are called "rationalists," and philosophers who hold that knowledge can be gained through experience are called "empiricists." Plato was a rationalist, and Aristotle was an empiricist. Plato held that our source of knowledge resides in the Ideas that we can recover or recollect if we try hard enough. In contrast, Aristotle held that we are born with a blank slate, so experience with the world is the source of knowledge.

Descartes was a rationalist who wanted to defeat skepticism, but in order to do so he had to find at least one idea of which he could be certain. He started by subjecting everything he formerly believed to a methodological doubt, meaning that if a belief did not pass the test of certainty, then it was rejected. A series of thought-experiments led Descartes to doubt not only what his senses offered, but also his beloved mathematical ideas, even something as simple as $2 + 2 = 4$.

How could he doubt that?

By invoking the possibility of an evil demon who had the power to trick Descartes at every turn. This powerful demon could be such that certainty would forever escape Descartes's grasp.

That's perverse.

Yes, but for Descartes, it was logically possible. And the sheer possibility is what drives skepticism and is what Descartes had to defeat.

If the demon can make all of Descartes's thoughts be mistaken, then there seems to be no hope for Descartes, or for us.

That is what Descartes was beginning to think, too. But then he hit upon something that he could not doubt, his famous "I think, therefore I am." Even if the content of everything he believed was false because the demon is forever tricking him, his being tricked means that he exists. So, whenever he has a thought, no matter if that thought is false, then he exists.

That's clever. Descartes defeated the evil demon. But was that enough to defeat skepticism?

For many people, no. Descartes not only wanted to find something of which he could be certain, he also wanted to get the rest of the world back. By that I mean he wanted to show that we have both a mind and a body, that a mental world and a physical world both exist and interact with each other. And on top of that he wanted to prove that God exists.

You mean from his one certainty, "I think, therefore I am," he could prove all that?

That was his goal. But he ran into trouble right from the start because it was quickly pointed out by others that even the way he structured his basic idea was flawed. Perhaps Descartes was not justified in using the word "I" because to claim that he would need to show that all the thoughts occurred in one being, namely him. But he had no way of knowing that; all he could do is say that thoughts exist, but where they were was not certain.

I see. Descartes's idea sounds right when you first hear it, but the criticism seems straightforward as well.

Descartes also gets credit—or blame, depending on your philosophical viewpoint—for setting up the modern mind-matter problem. As defined by Descartes, the mind is a mental substance that has no physical properties. Matter, being purely physical, is a non-mental substance. But once these two substances are separated a question immediately arises: How do they interact? This was a problem not only for Descartes, it still reverberates through philosophy and science nearly four hundred years later.

You mean no one has been able to figure it out?

Oh, there are lots of answers, but no consensus. If you think about it, the problem seems intractable. Once you posit a mind that is non-physical, you seem to create a barrier that cannot be crossed in either direction. For example, if you hold that the mind can cause bodily movements, then presumably this will be initiated somewhere in the brain. But we know how physical causes work, by one part of the physical world acting on another part of the physical world. For example, we can trace a pattern of brain activity, say through certain neurons firing, and observe an arm moving. A physical process leading to a physical effect. But how do we explain how my

259

mind, not my brain, can get even one neuron to fire? Where is the interface point and how does it work?

Doesn't my decision to move my arm cause it to move? And isn't that decision in my mind?

Exactly where thoughts and decisions exist are themselves not perfectly clear. A materialist can claim that those things are just complex brain processes, so there is no need to introduce a non-physical mental cause. Part of the discussion hinges on the term "cause" in that the normal way of using it is connected to the physical world. So, when we use the term to explain how a non-physical mind can affect a physical object, we take the term out of its normal application, setting us up for confusion. This confusion is realized in many avenues, such as movies. Although movies about ghosts can be enjoyed on many levels, they also introduce aspects that cannot be overlooked. For example, it is quite common to see a ghost in a movie walk through walls.

Sure, that is consistent with a ghost being non-physical.

It is consistent. But what is inconsistent is having that same ghost run or walk up steps. Do you see why?

I think so. In order for me to walk up steps, my foot has to push off each step. I can do

that because I have a physical body, but a
ghost can't because it has no physical parts.
So, yes, it is inconsistent to have the ghost
walk through walls but also walk up steps.
And now that I think about it, even walking
makes no sense. I mean we walk by touching
a floor or pavement, but a ghost couldn't
even do that. The ghost would just drift
through space.

And it gets no better when we think about how a ghost could see things in the physical world. We know that eyes require light waves to stimulate the act of seeing. But once again, a ghost should not be able to detect light waves because it has no sensory apparatus that can process the light waves.

Then the same thing holds for the mind. We
understand how light waves affect our eyes
and how signals are sent to the brain, but
how do all those physical processes make it
to the mind? I can see why it still interests
philosophers today.

Not only philosophers. Neuroscientists, biologists, cognitive scientists, and many others are also wrestling with the problem. The common-sense view is that we have a physical brain and a non-physical mind. This belief is captured in the philosophical theory called "dualism." Dualists claim that mental phenomena cannot be reduced to brain activity because experiences such as sensations, thoughts, and emotions are not just brain activity. For example, although scientists can observe what happens in my brain when I have the sensation of the color blue, they cannot observe my experience because the color I see is not available to anyone but me.

In contrast to dualism, the philosophical theory called "materialism" claims that reality is composed of nothing but matter. The main tenet is that all objects and events can be reduced to, or explained by, matter. For example, water is two parts hydrogen and one part oxygen. Materialists argue that sensations, thoughts, and everything else that dualists claim to be non-physical, including our consciousness, will eventually be explained when we get a comprehensive understanding of the complex brain functions.

Materialism is a reductionist theory, one that reduces mind-talk to brain-talk. For example, we can trace the movement of a finger through an elaborate cascade of muscle movement, nerve firings, and the brain activity that occurs in conjunction with the movement. Although a dualist claims that the movement was caused by a thought in the mind—"I will move my right index finger"—the materialist claims that once we fully understand all the involved brain functioning processes, then everything will be accounted for, so there will be nothing left over to explain. A major hurdle for dualism is to explain how the non-physical mind can cause the body to do anything; for example, how can the mind cause even one synapse to fire? There is a saying that sums up the issue between dualists and materialists: What is Mind? No Matter. What is Matter? Never Mind.

That's cute. I can see why the interaction problem is a difficult one for dualists.

Descartes ushered the mind-body problem into modern philosophy. Part of the problem stems from Descartes's definition of "mind" as a thinking substance, and "body" as an extended substance. The term "substance" is perfectly appropriate when we use it to refer to physical objects such as the brain; but it seems inappropriate when Descartes uses it to refer to the mind as a thinking substance. When we use the term "substance" to talk about the brain we understand the appropriateness of saying it has such things as weight, length, and color. It also has spatial coordinates, that is, we can specify where it exists in our body. We cannot say the same about the mind, because Descartes described it as not having any dimensions; no weight, no color, and no spatial coordinates. As such we cannot specify where it exists.

It must exist in the brain somewhere, although we do sometimes insult someone by telling him to get his head out of his butt.

I like graphic descriptions that get at the heart of the matter.

You managed to sneak in a lot by the phrase "the heart of the matter," since the heart is physical but the soul is not, and some people think the mind and soul are the same.

Many people do use the terms interchangeably, and they sometimes add consciousness into the mix. Even if we say the mind is somehow closely connected to the brain, we are still stuck with explaining what we mean by "connected." It just seems to push the problem back one step by saying that the mind somehow gets brain activity started. The question is how.

The philosopher, William James, argued that a lot of talk about consciousness, and the division of the world into thoughts and things, simply creates more confusion. His solution was to accept that the world is comprised of what he calls "pure experiences." For example, we can talk about an experience in a subjective way, by saying that "it represents." But we can also talk about that same experience in an objective way, by saying that "it is represented." It is James's contention that, as he put it, "What represents and what is represented is here numerically the same." If this is accepted, then dualism's breaking the world into two distinct substances is incorrect. But there is another aspect to James's "pure experiences" that is important. The philosopher, Thomas Nagel, wrote an influential article called "What is it Like to Be a Bat?"

That's a great title.

It is. Perhaps the way to get people to read your material is to come up with catchy titles. Nagel contends that any reductionist theory has to take into account the possibility that "an organism has conscious mental states if and only if there is something that it is to be that organism—something it is like for the organism."

Can you connect that to what James was saying?

Recall that James said the subjective and objective attitudes toward experiences are two ways of describing the same thing, that there are just pure experiences. Nagel claims that for any organism, not just humans, if there is something that it must be like to be that particular organism with those particular experiences, then that organism has consciousness.

So then a rock, for example, doesn't have consciousness because it doesn't have experiences that are unique to it.

We tend to think that a rock has no experiences in the sense that there is nothing at all to be like a rock. But if it makes sense to say there is something that it is like to be a human, or a bat, then that is what Nagel means by consciousness.

I think I got part of that, but maybe you can add more.

A more recent non-reductive theory, called "property dualism," tries to explain consciousness and give it a unique place in the world. The claim is that mental properties have emerged from the structure of the brain through the slow process of evolution, so that consciousness is a fundamental part of reality. Property dualists agree that a lot of human behavior can be explained by neuroscience and reduced to neural mechanisms. Nevertheless, they argue that "experience," in Nagel's sense of the word, cannot be explained in the same way because consciousness is not reducible to brain mechanisms or processes.

So, the property dualists argue that consciousness and experience are unique things that certain organisms have, but they are not identical to just what goes on in our brains. And these properties have emerged by way of evolution, so if life had evolved differently, then consciousness might never have existed. So, although consciousness is part of the world, it is unlike any physical part of the world. That seems to me to be a strong position.

As you might expect for any philosophical theory, it, too, has come under fire. One of its critics, the philosopher Patricia Churchland, argues that the apparent strength of property dualism rests on the state of our scientific knowledge. Churchland argues that whenever we lack scientific knowledge of a phenomenon, it simply points to us, not to the world at large. Churchland is arguing that throughout human history whenever people failed to understand how the world worked they created something to fill in the vacuum. For example, when science struggled to explain how life differed from inert objects, a theory called "vitalism" was proposed. The theory held that all living organisms have a non-physical force that gives them the property of life.

I took a biology course but I don't recall hearing about that theory.

I'm not surprised. The theory was abandoned once we could explain life without adding in an unnecessary ingredient. Churchland argues that property dualism may go the way of vitalism. Given this, her recommendation is that we wait to see how far neuroscience can take us to understanding consciousness. If we are eventually able to account for what are now the various functions attributed to consciousness, then we will have automatically accounted for experience. There would be nothing left over to explain.

Some philosophers tie consciousness to the question of personal identity, or an enduring self, the non-physical subject of consciousness. Is the self simply the totality of our memories and experiences, or because those things change over time, is the self an unchanging entity that houses temporary information about our life? In other words, what makes us unique persons? John Locke, defined "person" as a being in which consciousness is inseparable from thinking. For Locke, our personal identities depend exclusively on our consciousness.

So our bodies are not part of our personal identity, our self?

Correct. In fact, Locke, writing in the 1600s, was way ahead of his time because his idea that our personal identities depend exclusively on our consciousness led him to claim that if we could transfer our consciousness to another body, then that body would now be us.

He sounds like a science-fiction writer. I wonder what he would have thought about some books and movies that have used those ideas.

I suspect that he would enjoy them, once he got over the shock of seeing a movie. Notice that Locke's claim about our self moving from one body to the another is simply a consequence of how he defines consciousness. That is why philosophers place so much emphasis on seeing what follows from a given point. Once you commit to a premise then you should accept the logical consequences of your position. If not, then you should change your position.

That's a principle we should all follow. However, it seems that a lot of people, me included, are not quite willing to accept the logical consequences of our positions. We hold on to them even in the face of facts that go against us.

True. We are good at explaining away things that do not fit our preconceived notions and settled views. The term "ad hoc rescue" describes what people do when they are confronted with contradictory results. Since "ad hoc" means "whatever is needed," the person "rescues" the position by changing the parameters of the discussion to deflect the negative results. Since the facts that go against the position are now deemed to be irrelevant, the rescue ploy can be continuously applied.

I remember reading about a person who claimed that he could read other people's minds. A scientist got him to agree to do an experiment where the mind-reader would be in one room, and in another room a person would randomly draw a series of cards with numbers from 1-10 written on them. When a card was picked, the mind-reader was asked what number it was. The results showed that the mind-reader guessed correctly at about the same rate we would expect anyone else, around 10% correct guesses. Upon hearing this, the so-called mind reader said that his ability was hindered by the "negative waves" emanating from the skeptical scientist.

That is a perfect example of ad hoc rescue. His personal identity was bruised by the results, as it should have been.

Since our experiences change over time, we can ask how that affects the idea of an unchanging self. The writings of David Hume in the 1700s have influenced much of modern philosophy, and he offers us a different picture of the self from that of Locke. Hume said that although it is natural for us to firmly believe that we are intimately conscious of ourselves, nevertheless, we are mistaken. Since our experience consists of a constant succession of different sensations, it is impossible to derive a unique self from those ever-changing impressions. Hume captures this point powerfully when he says, "I never can catch myself at any time without a perception, and never can observe any thing but the perception." Hume tells us that, quite simply, what we call the self is just a bundle of different perceptions.

That's a wild idea. Surely I recognize myself through time. I admit that my life whizzes by, but something allows me to say that it all happens to me through my personal identity.

Hume's point is that there is a constant flux of perceptions, and nothing but a constant flux of perceptions. When we take that flux, and by reverse osmosis try to distill a self, Hume says that nothing is left.

If Hume is right about our personal identity and self, then does that mean there is no "I" who makes choices. Are both the "I" and free will just illusions?

Good questions. It seems natural for humans to have a strong belief in free will. If you offer me a choice of soup or salad, I seem in charge of my decision. I might even ask if I can have both. If a decision takes some time to make, then I seem to be aware of my deliberations, as I weigh the pros and cons of the choices available to me. But philosophers are not always swayed by the obvious. Nor are scientists. To our senses, nothing could be more obvious than the belief that the Earth does not move. But through the persistence of a few brave thinkers, we know that the Earth is not only round, it rotates on its axis, it revolves around the Sun, and our galaxy is moving, too. Even though this seems completely counterintuitive, most people have come to accept it.

And even though the belief in free will is so intuitive, some philosophers have persisted in challenging its existence.

Philosophers do not need to start out with a direct challenge to any idea, but their curiosity to investigate ideas leads them to see the consequences that follow from any belief.

> *So they push ideas to see if the ideas hold water, to see if they can find a weak spot or breaking point. Maybe philosophers are the quality control inspectors for the abstract products of our imaginations.*

I like that. And if they find serious flaws in the design, then we can try to correct the problems. When the Japanese film director, Akira Kurosawa, applied for a film school scholarship, the application asked him the following question: What are the fundamental problems with the Japanese film industry, and how can they be corrected? Kurosawa answered by saying that if the problems were fundamental, then they cannot be corrected.

> *That's a great answer. I assume he got the scholarship, but even if he didn't, he went on to direct many important films. I have admired his work for a long time.*

He was a great director and he influenced filmmakers around the world by rethinking how movies can be made. And as we saw, some philosophers are able to influence the way we think about things, too. The free will question does not live in a vacuum, it is entangled with the question of determinism. What motivated modern science was the belief that the natural world is subject to the principles of causality, the assumption that all physical events and processes can be understood through reason and experiments. Science rejects superstitions, magic potions, and gods that need our praise and sacrifices to ensure they will not be angry with us. Science progresses by a simple formula: All physical events can be explained by physical processes.

If determinism is correct, if everything in the physical world is determined by matter and the forces that act on it, and if we are nothing but physical beings, or as some have called us, "chemical bags," then at first blush, there seems to be no place for free will. Our bodies are completely subject to the laws of nature.

I agree that we are physical beings who are subject to the basic laws of nature, such as falling like a rock if thrown off a cliff, or dying if we are poisoned. Sorry to be so morbid. But can't we still argue that our consciousness provides us with the means to make at least some free choices, such as choosing either the soup or the salad? Why would that free choice violate the laws of nature?

Your choice does not violate the laws of nature, but if determinism is correct, then your choice did not derive from free will, it was the outcome of your entire physical past. If you think about it, our liking or disliking certain food or drinks is really subject to our taste buds, our sense of smell, texture, how we

273

digest things, and a host of other physical attributes that we were born with and over which we have no control. Paul-Henri d'Holbach added some spice to this idea. He said that although we seem to be consciously deliberating what to do, what is really going on inside our brains is the sorting out of conflicting physical forces acting on us that are temporarily not strong enough in any direction to get us to act. When the causal forces finally line up in one direction, we act.

> *But I can train myself to like something. I mean, most people don't immediately like the taste or smell of cigarettes, but they can persist in smoking until they do.*

True enough. Humans have a strange capacity for tolerating many things that are bad for them. But that capacity is most likely built into us through our DNA. Many behaviors, such as alcoholism and drug addiction have been connected to certain DNA sequences, meaning that those people are more likely to become addicted. And this is where the environment plays a part, too. If you grow up in a place where alcohol or cigarettes do not exist, then the potential for addiction to those things is zero.

> *That's the old nature versus nurture debate. According to determinism, even though your physical makeup predisposes you to an addiction, it isn't necessarily your destiny to become addicted. There has to be an*

opportunity to come in contact with the addictive material. I'm amazed by all the complicated connections between free will, consciousness, and determinism, so much so that one cannot be answered without the others. And I'm really flummoxed by the self and personal identity problems.

I share much of your perplexity. I have often found myself attracted to a position, only to discover at a later time that someone has written either a strong critique of that position, or has offered a completely new alternative. But that is one reason why I find philosophy so fascinating.

Our free will may be simply the physical ability to act in a certain way. We have a tendency to talk about most animals as acting on instinct, meaning their the acts are determined solely by their physical nature, that their actions are programmed or hard-wired. Perhaps what we call free will is simply the physical ability to bring about a particular act. Baruch Spinoza argued that everything in nature proceeds by necessity, that our so-called free will decisions are really determined by underlying physical causes. And since every cause has a prior cause, there is no end to the causal links.

Now Spinoza adds the issue of an infinite chain of cause and effects to our already crowded scene.

Your choice of the word "scene" is appropriate, and it echoes Shakespeare's phrase "All the world's a stage, and all the men and women merely players." We are like characters in a play who merely follow what has already been written. And that brings us back to Hume and personal identity.

I'm glad you brought that up. I wanted to ask if Hume put his name on his books.

Yes, he did.

Aha! Then Hume must have thought he constituted a unique self, that he had a personal identity. If so, then isn't he contradicting himself?

Hume is not questioning our use of a name to identify ourselves, he is saying that the persistent psychological pull of self-identity does not provide the grounds for the metaphysical belief in an enduring self, as a thing that exists independently of our fleeting perceptions. Hume says "I may venture to affirm of the rest of mankind, that they are nothing but a bundle or collection of different perceptions, which succeed each other with an inconceivable rapidity, and are in a perpetual flux and movement. Our eyes cannot turn in their sockets without varying our perceptions. Our thought is still more variable than our sight; and all our other senses and faculties contribute to this change; nor is there any single power of the soul, which remains unalterably the same, perhaps for one moment. The mind is a theatre, where several perceptions successively make their appearance; pass, re-pass, glide away, and mingle in an infinite variety of postures and situations. There is properly no simplicity in it at one time, nor identity in different, whatever natural propension we may have to imagine that simplicity and identity. The comparison of the theatre must not mislead us. They are the successive perceptions only that constitute the mind; nor have we the most distant notion of the place where these scenes are represented, or of the materials of which it is composed."

That is really quite beautiful, vivid and compelling. But surely the question of whether we have free will affects our ethical questions about moral responsibility and punishment. I imagine that most, if not all, societies believe that young children aren't morally responsible for their behavior. Although the cut-off age probably varies in different societies, I suspect the determining factor is when they think that we become capable of rationally understanding right and wrong actions. And although we sometimes put down a dog who killed a person, it isn't because we think the dog committed a morally wrong act. The dog is the cause of the death, but it is not morally responsible. If humans don't have free will, then we are like that dog; if I kill someone, then I caused the death, but I am not morally responsible.

That is a fine way of connecting free will, moral responsibility, and punishment. And we already saw that we have to add consciousness into the mix. And perhaps personal identity will be an exotic spice that we can add for additional taste. Free will is intimately connected with conscious deliberations. Hume offers an idea about how we make moral judgments. Although Hume was not a scientist in the modern sense, he grounded his thoughts on an empirical investigation into our behavior. In fact, a lot of Hume's ideas can be viewed through a psychological lens. For example, he tells us that moral decisions are not based on reason because reason deals only with facts; therefore, reason cannot determine whether to choose one moral option over another.

Reason plays no part in our moral actions? Then what part does reason play?

Hume puts in quite succinctly when he tell us that "Reason is, and ought only to be the slave of the passions, and can never pretend to any other office than to serve and obey them."

If reason just helps us to get the job done, to put it crudely, then all our decisions and actions stem from our passions, our primal urges. Where does morality fit in?

278

For Hume, "morality is determined by sentiment. It defines virtue to be whatever mental action or quality gives to a spectator the pleasing sentiment of approbation; and vice the contrary." What we call morality is simply our feelings of approval or disapproval. For example, approval can take the form of praise for a certain act, while disapproval can take the form of blame for an act. It rests on our passions, our emotional reactions to an action.

> *You said that Hume took an empirical position, so his theory is the physics of morality: For every moral action there is a moral reaction.*

Well done. Do you mind if I use that someday?

> *Not at all. I'm flattered that you like it. You mentioned the psychological aspect of Hume's thoughts. Can this be connected to Freud's conceptions of the Id, Ego, and Superego? I mean, it seems like the Id is what Hume calls the passions, but then the Superego seems to fit that, too. I'm not sure about the Ego.*

The Id would be the driving force behind an action, and if the action is deemed to have moral implications, then the Superego would play the part of the spectator assessing whether the action merits approval or disapproval. Translating Freud's terms once again into Hume's arena, the Ego looks out on the world and it deals with facts and patterns, but although it plays the part of reason, it can only feed information to the passions, so in that sense it does not contribute directly to moral decisions. But since it controls our bodies, the Id, the passions, rely on the Ego to get the job done, as you so colorfully put it.

> *It seems to me that Hume places morality in a strange position. There doesn't seem to be a place for objective morality, or morality that cuts across time. I guess I mean that it seems to lead to nihilism, at least what little I know of that concept; something like the abandonment of moral or religious principles; a belief that life has no meaning, so anything goes.*

Ah, the old Cole Porter song. How does it go? Something like "In olden days, a glimpse of stocking was looked on as something shocking, but now, God knows, anything goes." Catchy tune. I do not know whether Cole Porter read anything by Friedrich Nietzsche, but the sentiment is familiar. Although Nietzsche is often associated with nihilism, that characterization is misguided. Nietzsche outlines the history of human societies, starting with a "pre-moral society," characterized by the belief that the moral value of an act is determined strictly by its consequences. Humans then moved on to a "moral society," characterized by the belief that the moral value of an act is determined by the motive behind the act. Nietzsche urges us to understand that we need to overcome morality by accepting that our conscious intentions are merely the surface appearance of the drives that determine our actions.

That sounds a lot like Hume.

It does. But Nietzsche goes where Hume might have feared to tread. The conclusion of Nietzsche's argument about morality is that we must strive for independence from morality and religion. We must free ourselves from the chains of outdated beliefs so we can become free spirits.

Chapter 22

INDIVIDUALS

As a species, humans seem to struggle with competing desires: to be independent and to belong to a group. These struggles led to the creation of small tribes and to massive civilizations where rules of behavior are decided and the debate over how much individual freedom can be tolerated. Thomas Hobbes captured the human predicament when he said that our lives are "solitary, poor, nasty, brutish, and short."

Ouch, that's harsh.

Perhaps Hobbes should have added "harsh" to the mix. Sorry, I had to say that, but I understand what you mean. Hobbes's devastating description of our lives provides an impetus for humans to create a social contract, whereby we agree to some combination of individual rights and duties. The rights protect our individual freedom, and the duties protect us from those who break the laws. According to Hobbes, a social contract is necessary because without it we will always act in our own self-interest.

If there is no social contract, then might makes right.

If there is no social contract, then perhaps rights do not exist. In that case might simply makes actual.

But doesn't the idea of a social contract assume the concept of human freedom, including the ability to make choices. So we're back to free will and consciousness and the self. Philosophy does spiral back on itself. You can't solve one thing without it causing you to deal with a lot of other things. No wonder it's so hard.

But it is fun. Of course, my definition of "fun" may seem perverse to others. And my having a definition of "fun" that is quite expansive is also fun to me.

Okay, now that's just weird.

I was going to say that "weird" can also be fun. In fact, I just said it. But you are correct that we seem forced to deal with interconnected ideas, such as agreeing to a social contract implies free will directed toward goals, such as living in a safe society. So, why would anyone be willing to give up freedom? If Hobbes is right about the stark nature of our lives, then for many people the tradeoff is an easy choice.

The trick, then, is to balance some degree of individual freedom with some degree of

*constraint on our individual desires. No
wonder laws change over time. People once
believed that alcohol consumption caused
many social problems, so Prohibition was
enacted. Of course, since that ultimately led
to severe unexpected consequences, it was
repealed. Over time the pendulum seems to
sweep from maximizing individual freedom
back toward maximizing constraints on
behavior.*

We are living through another era where this is being
played out, the rise of social media. The question of
free speech has been debated for thousands of years.
Socrates was condemned to death because he was
judged to have corrupted the youth, and to have
denied the existence of the Greek gods.

In the 1800s, John Stuart Mill held that freedom
of thought and open discussion of ideas and opinions
is a necessity for democratic societies. The internet
and social media are putting Mill's ideas to the test.
In the 1900's, John Dewey reminded us that
democracy is a way of life; it requires active
participation and a commitment to cooperation.
Dewey said that "unless democratic habits of thought
and action are part of the fiber of a people, political
democracy is insecure." The fragile nature of
democracy is currently being tested in many parts of
the world.

Chapter 23

DEFENSES

*Since you mentioned Socrates again, I was
hoping we have enough time to talk about
him before the train reaches my stop.*

There is a lot to talk about, but we can get started and
see how far we get. A good way to start discussing
Socrates is to understand that he did not write
anything, so we have only the reports of others to
guide us. But we know that Socrates talked a lot. His
conversations regarding the most important
questions of life had a profound influence on
philosophy. A lot of what we know about Socrates
comes from the writings of Plato who tried to capture
the essence of Socrates's thoughts in the form of
dialogues.

*I have heard the term "Socratic method,"
but can you give me a short explanation of
it?*

The term comes from the technique in which
Socrates poses a series of probing questions to a
person claiming to have knowledge of a

philosophical topic. The process often results in Socrates showing that his conversation partner's ideas lead to an untenable position. This method of inquiry, called "elenchus," is a form of cross-examination that Socrates often used to explore the logical consequences of certain positions to see if they stand up under scrutiny. To the enemies of Socrates the phrase "probing questions" is too mild—they describe what Socrates did as intimidating, infuriating, and humiliating. In Socrates's defense, he engaged only those who had either a reputation for wisdom, or those who claimed to know something with certainty. Given this, it is not surprising to hear that Socrates was revered by many young people who became his followers and who typically enjoyed seeing arrogance deflated and defeated. Socrates's precise questioning of the wisdom pretenders can also be described as afflicting the comforted.

Can you give me some biographical information about Socrates?

The bare bones of Socrates's life can be sketched as follows: He was born in 469 BCE—before the common era—and died in 399 BCE; he served in the Athenian army; he fought in three battles; he was married to Xanthippe, and he had three sons. It is not clear how Socrates earned a living since he denied taking money for teaching; he lived during tumultuous political times and he had powerful enemies; he was put on trial for corrupting the youth and irreverence toward the gods; he was found guilty and sentenced to death by poisoning; he drank a potion of hemlock that caused his death.

What did Socrates question people about? What were some of his beliefs, and why have his ideas continued to interest people for so long?

The best way to figure that out is to read Plato's writings. Plato often created his own philosophical body of work by expanding on Socrates's ideas. Plato's writings amount to around two thousand pages, the importance of which was captured by the philosopher Alfred Whitehead, when he remarked that Western philosophy "consists of a series of footnotes to Plato."

If you like, we can look at Socrates's trial since that shines light on much of Socrates's life. It reveals a person deeply absorbed with clarifying the important issues of life. Socrates was a willing partner in the search for truth, virtue, knowledge, and wisdom. In fact, his willingness to spend as much time as necessary in trying to understand those concepts shows Socrates's utmost respect for other people's beliefs.

Let me say something about the title of Plato's dialogue about the trial. It is called *Apology*. Today the word is used most often to express remorse or regret for having done something wrong. The Greek word "apologia" meant a speech given in one's defense; thus when Plato used the term, his contemporaries understood what this meant. Even though the term has a different meaning today, philosophers kept the title *Apology*.

Why was Socrates put on trial, and why was he executed?

As I mentioned earlier, he was indicted on the charges of corrupting the youth of Athens, and irreverence toward the gods. The charges against Socrates were brought out in court. As was the custom, the accusers went first and provided their testimony. The jury system was quite unlike what we have today. Whereas we generally have 12 jurors, the Athenian jury in Socrates's case consisted of approximately 500 citizens who would cast a vote in the matter. When it was Socrates's turn to address the court, he started by saying that he kept looking around to see who his accusers were talking about since nothing they said about him was true.

That's an ironic way of starting.

Yes, and it showed that although the charges were quite serious, Socrates was not about to be intimidated by the accusations. He said that his accusers had warned the jurors to be careful of being deceived by the force of Socrates's eloquence. In reply to this, Socrates said that he pledged to to speak truthfully, and asked the jurors to decide justly. The jurors can then decide if speaking the plain truth is eloquent.

Socrates said that his current accusers were simply echoing the opinions of enemies whose false charges started long ago. They claimed that Socrates practiced sophistry, the art of winning an argument by using deceitful and fallacious methods. Those old false accusations got passed around by those who were on the losing side of a conversation. Instead of admitting that their positions did not hold up under scrutiny, they claimed that Socrates used deceitful methods against them.

So, Socrates was aware that his long-standing bad reputation among many citizens, and the rumors surrounding him, might prejudice some jurors against him.

That is right.

How could he possibly diffuse or even fight against any prejudice among the jurors?

That was a difficult challenge. Socrates said that he was not a sophist because he never asked for or received any money for instruction. His accusers had provided no witnesses or evidence to support that charge. Socrates then proceeded to tell the story of his bad reputation and how it all started by his being called "wise." Socrates said that his life's work resulted from a chance occurrence. One of Socrates's friends went to the Temple of Apollo at Delphi and asked the Oracle whether there was anyone wiser than Socrates.

The Oracle speaks for Apollo?

The belief was that under the right conditions Apollo would sometimes make pronouncements through the Oracle who resided at the temple. The Oracle was reported to have said that no one was wiser than Socrates. Upon hearing this, Socrates was puzzled because he felt that he did not possess any real wisdom. But since a god such as Apollo would not lie, Socrates interpreted the pronouncement as being a riddle.

Why did Socrates call the Oracle's answer a "riddle"?

Socrates knew that the Oracle sometimes spoke in such a way that the pronouncement could be interpreted several ways. You might have heard the story of Croesus who sent someone to Delphi to ask the Oracle whether he should go to war against the Persian Empire. The Oracle replied: "If Croesus goes to war, he will destroy a great empire." Croesus was happy to hear this, so he went to fight the Persian army. The Oracle's pronouncement was correct, but it was Croesus's empire that was destroyed.

I see how Croesus might have interpreted the statement as indicating that he would win. So, the Oracle's statements, although believed to come from Apollo, are subject to multiple interpretations.

Correct, and it is why Socrates thought maybe the Oracle's statement was a riddle that he had to solve. Socrates told the jurors that he devised a method to unravel the riddle. He would search for someone who was truly wise, and upon finding that person Socrates could then go to the Oracle and ask for an explanation of the riddle.

Did Socrates find someone?

We shall see. Socrates started his search by going to a politician who was famous for being wise. After having engaged the politician in conversation, Socrates determined that the politician possessed no real wisdom. This dismayed Socrates for several reasons. First, Socrates had hoped the politician would be wise so he could go to the Oracle with this information. Second, after Socrates had exposed the politician as a person who contradicted himself, the politician, having been embarrassed in front of his followers, turned his scorn on Socrates and, helped by his followers, began spreading rumors about Socrates. Upon reflection, Socrates thought that although neither he nor the politician possessed any real and useful knowledge, perhaps Socrates is better off than the politician because the politician knows nothing but still believes he is wise, while Socrates neither knows nor think that he is wise.

At the end of his conversation with the

politician, Socrates realized that neither of them really knew anything. The politician is deluded because he knows nothing, but thinks that he knows. Socrates doesn't delude himself—he knows nothing, but does not think that he knows. So, in that sense Socrates is wiser than the politician. Maybe the Oracle was right, after all.

Perhaps. Socrates continued his defense at the trial by telling of his long search for a wise person. In fact. Socrates spent the rest of his life—he lived to be over seventy—searching and questioning everyone who was willing to talk.

I can understand why he had so many enemies.

Indeed. But as he told the jurors, he was simply following the pronouncement of Apollo.

That was smart because it showed that Socrates's behavior was in line with his reverence toward Apollo. He was wise to use this as a way to refute the charge of irreverence toward the gods.

That was Socrates's intent. By showing that he diligently and dutifully followed the Oracle's pronouncement, Socrates revealed his reverence toward Apollo. Socrates's defense at this point was his way of explaining what he believed to be the correct way to live a just and honorable life. He told the court that since he devoted his life to searching for wisdom, he had no time for politics or having a regular occupation; thus he lives in poverty due to his devotion to Apollo.

Socrates continued to show his obedience to Apollo by conversing with anyone willing to discuss important topics. But unfortunately, his obedience explains why he had so many enemies. It's not surprising that many people would hate him. Nobody likes to be exposed as a "wisdom fraud." Especially those who have a reputation in the community.

That is a good way of putting it. Socrates proceeded to describe other reasons for his bad reputation. He had many young followers, many who came from wealthy families, so they had free time to tag along and observe Socrates's conversations. Those young people sometimes tried to mimic Socrates's methods of examining people's beliefs. Not surprisingly, this resulted in those who were embarrassed becoming angry with Socrates. This, Socrates told the jurors, was the origin of the charges that Socrates was a corrupter of youth.

As if being embarrassed by Socrates wasn't enough, they had to put up with their children questioning their authority and calling their bluff, so to speak.

Yes, that would be a growing source of irritation to the older people, especially those with a reputation they would like to see remain untarnished. When Socrates's young followers imitated his style of questioning, the elders accused Socrates of being an evil teacher and corrupting the youth.

After explaining the history of his search for the answer to the Oracle's statement, and the reputation he gained by questioning others, Socrates then turned his attention to one of his main accusers, a young man by the name of Meletus. Earlier in his testimony, Meletus told the court that Socrates was evil because he corrupted the youth of Athens, and that Socrates did not believe in the gods of the state, and he has created other new gods of his own. Socrates proceeded to expose Meletus as a liar.

Socrates said that he would show that Meletus was the one who did evil because he makes a joke of a serious matter. Meletus brought Socrates to trial under false pretenses, from a fake interest about matters in which he was not really concerned. Socrates asked Meletus if he spent a lot of time thinking about the improvement of the youth. Meletus answered that he had. Socrates asked him to explain who it is that improves the youth. Meletus was silent for a while, so Socrates prompted him again. Meletus was embarrassed and he stumbled for an answer; he blurted out that the laws improve the youth. Socrates pointed out that Meletus's answer missed the point and avoided Socrates's meaning. Socrates asked Meletus to indicate specifically who the persons are who know the laws, and by having that knowledge, they are capable of improving the youth. Meletus answer was that the judges who are present in court are the ones. Socrates then asked if all the judges, or only some of them are capable of instructing and improving the youth. Meletus asserted that, of course, all the judges were capable of improving the youth.

> *Meletus sure knew how to suck up to the court. He knew the judges would be flattered by his response.*

I agree. I imagine him as a smarmy character, squirming under Socrates's questioning. But Socrates forced Meletus to double-down on his flattery. Socrates asked if the jurors also improve the youth. Meletus said that of course they do. Socrates widened the scope and asked if perhaps the citizens of Athens corrupt the youth. Meletus said that all the citizens improve the youth. Socrates said that if what Meletus claimed was true, then he, Socrates was the only corrupter of the youth. Meletus said that is the truth.

> *That claim is laughable. Did Meletus really expect the jurors to believe that of the thousands of citizens no one but Socrates was a corrupter of the youth?*

Recall that many of the jurors were already against Socrates. Given that, no matter how absurd

Meletus's claims were, many jurors would not be swayed by Socrates having exposed Meletus as a liar. Especially the jurors who were themselves exposed as wisdom frauds, or those who knew of someone who had been.

Socrates then proceeded to question Meletus about the charge that Socrates corrupted the young by teaching them not to acknowledge the gods recognized by the state, but instead, some other new spiritual agencies. Socrates said that he did not understand whether Meletus was asserting whether Socrates taught people to acknowledge some gods, so he was not an atheist, or whether Meletus was asserting that Socrates was an atheist and a teacher of atheism. Meletus took the bait and said that Socrates was an atheist.

Socrates admonished Meletus once again as a liar, and that Meletus contradicted himself. Socrates asked whether anyone could believe both in the existence of humans and not in the existence of humans. Meletus refused to answer, so Socrates answered that no one ever believed those things. Continuing this line of questioning, Socrates asked whether someone could believe in spiritual agencies, but not in spirits or demigods. Meletus admitted that it was not possible. Socrates continued by stating that Meletus had sworn in his indictment that Socrates taught people to believe in new spiritual agencies. This was the contradiction that Socrates was looking for. Earlier, Meletus had claimed that Socrates was an atheist, but now he claimed that Socrates taught people to believe in new spiritual agencies.

Socrates destroyed the credibility of his main accuser. His cross-examining was terrific. He had the young man tied up in knots, and made him appear foolish. It was silly of Meletus to say that everyone but Socrates improves the youth, or that he didn't believe in gods, especially after the story about Socrates's reverence toward Apollo.

Socrates made sure the jurors understood the full import of what had happened. He pointed out that Meletus's testimony was not only foolish, it illustrated the emptiness of the accusations. Socrates's cross-examination did two things: it revealed the truth and exposed the accusations as false. Socrates then asked the jurors to consider that when the truth is revealed, is anyone corrupted?

That was clever. Since Socrates was on trial for corrupting the youth, the cross-examination of Meletus simply revealed the truth, so how could that be a corrupting influence?

Yes. Socrates said that using our ability to reason is in fact a liberating force because it reveals the truth. He told the jurors that this was the path that he followed in his public discussions.

Socrates knew that exposing Meletus as a liar would not sway those who were dead set against him, so he had to try convincing those who were still open-minded. To those who thought that his life pursuit seemed destined to end in his making enemies, Socrates said that we should consider only whether our actions are right or wrong. If he had feared death more than an honest search for truth, then he would have abandoned Apollo. If that were the case, then the accusations that he denied the existence of the gods would have been justified. A fear of death assumes knowledge of the unknown. Socrates said that whereas he knew nothing of the afterworld, he did not pretend that he did.

> *Maybe that is a kind of wisdom. Of course, most of us fear the unknown, especially the prospect of our death. But I understand why Socrates used this to show that if his reverence to Apollo lead to his death, then he would rather suffer the consequences than abandon Apollo.*

Socrates then did an interesting thing. In order to get the jurors to think about how they will vote, Socrates said that every fair-minded person would agree that injustice is dishonorable. And since he has clearly shown that the accusations against him were unfounded, then perhaps some of the jurors will say to Socrates that we will acquit you, but on one condition: you must stop questioning everyone you meet. If you do not, then we will find ourselves back in court, and most likely you will be sentenced to die.

Socrates said that would require him to abandon

298

his duty to Apollo. That duty required him to question those whose life's interest was in acquiring money, power, and fame, instead of wisdom, truth and improving their characters. Socrates said to either acquit him or find him guilty. In either case, he will never change his way of life, not even if he has to die many times.

> *Maybe I'm hearing this incorrectly, but it sure seems that Socrates is defying the court to find him guilty. He tells them straight out that if they let him off, he will continue to act the same way.*

Socrates is nothing if not consistent. After all, he has been accused of not believing in the gods. Socrates argued that not only does he believe in gods, his reverence compels him to continue to follow the pronouncement of Apollo, even if it should lead to his death. In fact, Socrates anticipated your concern. He said that if they kill him, then they will have harmed themselves more than him because they would have proven to be dishonorable persons. This is so because the greatest evil is to unjustly take away another person's life.

Socrates then said that he is a gift to the citizens. He compared himself to a gadfly that was given to the people by Apollo. Socrates asked the jurors to imagine the state as a large sluggish horse, and Socrates is the gadfly. All day long he lands on the horse, biting, annoying, and provoking you. You may feel irritated and think that if you kill the gadfly, then you would be able to sleep without being stirred to action.

> *Socrates's comparing himself to a fly is great. Flies can definitely be annoying, and they do arouse us, at least enough to shoo them away. But, if we are really annoyed, we kill them. So maybe the analogy will backfire.*

Perhaps he is once again illustrating his consistent behavior. Even at this point, during a trial where his life is at stake, he does not take the easy way out. He continues to stir people to think about important things, even if they might not want to. Socrates said that some people want to know why so many others delight in conversing with him. It was true that some, young and old, like to hear his cross-examinations—there can be a sort of amusement in this. But that is not why he did it. If he really corrupted the youth, then there should be witnesses to that. Socrates asked them to come forward and swear to the court. No one came forward. Then perhaps some of the relatives of those he supposedly corrupted would be willing to relate the evil their families suffered at his hands. Now is their time. Let them present themselves as witnesses against him. Again, no one came forward to testify against him

> *That no one came forward to support the accusers should really help Socrates's case. After all, if he was supposed to have*

300

damaged so many people for so many years, then there should be lots of people willing to testify against him.

Right. But of course, after seeing how Socrates embarrassed Meletus, do you think that they would want to be exposed in public once again?

I didn't think of that. If Socrates had already shown that they are pretenders to wisdom then they surely would not want to be exposed in public court by his devastating cross-examination. That was smart of Socrates to call them out.

Socrates was just about finished with his defense. He said that some people on trial had brought family members to plead for mercy. Others had used flowery speech; some had resorted to sophistry to try confusing the jurors. Socrates said that it is wrong and harmful to win acquittal by using means other than convincing arguments, evidence, and speaking the truth. Thus, the jurors should not expect him to do anything dishonorable, especially since he is being tried for irreverence. Socrates ended his defense by saying, "To you and to god I commit my cause, to be determined by you as is best for you and me."

I understand why Socrates said that he wanted to win acquittal only by using convincing arguments, evidence, and reason. That is what his life's work has been all about. But once again, he seems to deliberately provoke and embarrass some of the jurors. I mean, he is right to criticize people who use pity to get themselves off or to minimize their punishment, especially if they are guilty. But he does it in a way that can seem like an accusation against some of the people he needs to be on his side.

There are many ways to interpret Socrates's defense. Some of the questions you raise point to several possible motivations behind Socrates's strategy. For example, he seems at times to be daring the jury to convict him.

Yes, it seems like he wants to be a martyr.

Some people have suggested that possibility. Others have said that perhaps Socrates realized that he was getting old and that he did not want to suffer a long period of painful inactivity awaiting death. It has also been pointed out that since Athens had been experiencing political upheavals, severe infighting, and political instability for a number of years, Socrates's enemies wanted to eliminate his influence. At least that could explain some of the motivation for his enemies to bring Socrates to trial. What is clear is that Socrates's defense was a powerful combination of reason and provocation. His defiance can also be viewed as another instance of his constant desire to wake people up from their slumber and get them to think about life.

What happened next?

The jury voted and Socrates was found guilty. He said that he was not saddened by the vote, that he expected it, and he was surprised that the votes were so nearly equal. He thought that the majority against him would have been much larger, and that if thirty votes out of the five hundred had gone over to the other side, he would have been acquitted. His accusers proposed death as the punishment. As was the custom of the court, Socrates had to offer a counter-proposal.

Socrates asked what should be done to someone who willingly gave up what most people desire; money, luxury, or political power. Instead he spent his life trying do the greatest good to everyone he met by convincing them to seek virtue and wisdom. Therefore, he should receive the reward due to him. He should receive free meals in the state dining room, the place reserved for the most distinguished citizens.

Please tell me that Socrates didn't really say that. Did he seriously think that the same jurors who had just found him guilty would reward him?

I will let Socrates answer for himself. He realized that many jurors would find his proposal insulting. But, argued Socrates, since he never intentionally wronged anyone, why would he wrong himself? He said that he does not deserve any punishment or penalty. Socrates then said that perhaps the jury would accept a proposal for imprisonment instead of the death penalty. Socrates rejected that by pointing out that he did not deserve to be a slave of temporary rulers. Socrates said that perhaps he should propose the penalty to be a fine, and imprisonment until the fine is paid. In that case, Socrates would have to spend a lot of time in prison because he had no money. Socrates then said that perhaps his penalty should be exile, which would have been a way for the jury to eliminate Socrates without having him put to death. Socrates dismissed that possibility since if his own countrymen could not put up with him, then others would not likely welcome him.

Socrates seems to be eliminating any possibility of leniency.

It seems that way, but Socrates was not finished. He said that maybe some of the jurors were thinking to themselves, "Socrates, no one will interfere with you if you simply learn to hold your tongue!" To this Socrates said, once again, that doing so would be a disobedience to a divine command, something that he would not do. Here is where Socrates said something that encapsulates his life: "The unexamined life is not worth living."

That does capture perfectly his profound belief, and it points to his never-ending quest for truth and why he tried to help others. Nevertheless, I, too, want to say to Socrates, "Can't you just hold your tongue and no one will bother you?" I feel conflicting emotions. I understand his reasons for living his life as he did, and I want him to go unpunished, but I can respect and admire his amazing consistency in reasoning, no matter what the consequences.

Many people feel conflicted and frustrated as you do. Perhaps we admire courageous people who are willing to die for their beliefs, knowing that we probably can never match that courage.

Then what happened?

The jury voted on the punishment and condemned Socrates to death. Socrates was allowed to make a final comment to the court. Socrates first addressed the jurors who voted for the death penalty. If they hoped that by eliminating Socrates they would not have to account for their lives, then they were mistaken. Instead of killing him, they should try to improve themselves. Their vote for the death penalty revealed themselves as dishonorable persons.

Socrates then addressed those who voted for acquittal. He said that perhaps death is a journey of the soul to another world. If so, then we might meet those who were virtuous and wise in life. If so, then I will be able to continue my search for knowledge because in that world they do not put a man to death for this.

Socrates then said that maybe death is a state of nothingness and unconsciousness. If there is no consciousness after death, then it is like a sleep undisturbed even by dreams. If so, then consider how pleasant such a night can be. If death is like this, then death is a gift, because eternity will be only a single night.

The way that Socrates puts it, that either death is like an eternal unconscious sleep, or else a migration of our soul from this world to a better place, sounds comforting. Still, there is something deep inside me that does not want my life to end too soon. Would Socrates criticize me for feeling that way?

Socrates's entire defense was to look upon life as a constructive force. Do you recall Socrates's words, "the unexamined life is not worth living"?

Yes.

As long as you spend your life asking the right questions, instead of just pursuing riches or fame, then Socrates would not be critical. He, of all people, knew how difficult it is to achieve knowledge and wisdom. He attacks pretenders of truth, wisdom frauds, and he is highly critical of those who fritter their life away pursuing transitory rewards. He probably thought that he lived the best life he could, and for a long enough time.

Finally, we should recognize that Socrates saw his being condemned to death as an act of injustice by men who were threatened by his existence. Although Socrates's actions and defense may have helped bring about his death, we must acknowledge that he stayed true to his beliefs. If he suddenly changed his way of searching for the truth in order to save himself, then this would be an admission that his life was a sham.

Chapter 24

MEANINGS

What happened at Socrates's trial was frustrating to hear, but at the same time it also made clear his life and his beliefs. Okay, I think I'm ready for this one: Does life have meaning?

A big question with multiple layers to unpack. One layer might be whether human life is intrinsically meaningful. If it is, then does it already exist at birth, or does it arise in the course of a life? Is it tied to accomplishments, behavior, character, or moral acts which depend on interactions with others. Can a solitary life have meaning? Can a mass murderer have lived a meaningful life? Can a life lived in constant hunger and pain be meaningful? Do we slice up a person's life and weigh only certain pieces on a scale?

Again with the tough questions. If I have to figure out the answers to all those questions, then the phrase "a meaningful life" is really complicated.

Did you think it would be simple? Many people look for an answer that can be put on a post-it note and stuck on the refrigerator for easy access. Recall that I said there are multiple layers to unpack. We are barely at the beginning.

I was afraid you would say that. Go on.

Can we weigh or judge the value of one life against another; in other words, is one person's life more meaningful than another person? If so, then how can we square that with the idea that all lives are intrinsically meaningful? Do we gain or lose some of the intrinsic nature depending on how our lives play out? Is whether I live a meaningful life contingent on where or when I exist, or is the intrinsic nature a universally objective feature of human existence?

Many people believe that life can have meaning only if God exists, so is any talk of an intrinsic nature bound up with God's existence?

It is possible to bypass the intrinsic question by using phrases such as "an influential life," or "a significant life," or simply "an interesting life." That might allow us to concentrate on the contingencies that affect our lives, allowing us to talk about a person's life by reference to the particular facts surrounding that person's existence.

So how we judge the significance of someone's life, or the worth of that life, or even whether that person lived an interesting life, would depend on the criteria we agree to apply to each case. But that seems dependent on time and place. Unless there is a universal standard of assessment—which I'm doubting now— short of total acceptance of, and devout faith in, an established religion.

Bringing God back into the question, the philosopher, Søren Kierkegaard, maintained that life has meaning in a certain relationship with God that is possible only if we have an eternal consciousness, the absence of which would doom us to a life of despair. In other words, for Kierkegaard, if death leads to oblivion, then life is empty. But it seems possible for life to have meaning without God. We are aware of pain and suffering, and we are also aware of life's joys when they happen and when we remember them. These are as real as it gets for mere mortals. That they are fleeting and may eventually dissolve as the universe runs down, should not detract from their immediate effect. A simple act of kindness may not have any eternal meaning, but it does not follow that the immediate real experience, deep feelings, and future memories of the act have no meaning.

I am psychologically attracted to the idea that meaning can exist within a life, but it is still hard for me to separate my inner

feelings from thinking that some external
relation must also exist.

Can you spell that out a bit more?

I'll try. Let's go back to Socrates's life. I
agree that his life was meaningful, but part
of the reason I say that is that his story has
been told for a few thousand years. I
wonder what would have happened had no
one written about him. Does his being
remembered provide a necessary ingredient
to what it means to be meaningful?

Are you suggesting that unless we are remembered,
our life might not have meaning? Is that what you
mean by it being a necessary ingredient?

That's why I said that I am psychologically
torn. I'll give you another example. There
are some movies that have characters who
affect those around them. I'm thinking of
Cool Hand Luke, or The Wild Bunch. The
stories are memorable to me because I was
caught up in their lives, but then the endings
seem to say that everything they did lead
nowhere. Their lives, even though fictional,
stay with me, so in that sense they have
meaning. But since I and everyone else who
remembers those movies will eventually be
gone as the universe winds down, then the

meaning seems to be completely bound up with remembrances.

I also have strong memories of the two movies that you mentioned. There is another movie that I saw at a young age, *The Incredible Shrinking Man*. The main character gets smaller and smaller. He is confronted with the knowledge that he will soon be insignificantly small as he approaches oblivion. But the entire time he is shrinking he is confronted with huge survival obstacles forcing him to come to grips with an everchanging landscape to which he must adapt. His overcoming of the obstacles made me think that he lived a fascinating life, so I was not sad at the ending. But later in life I came across other people who saw the movie and they said it made them depressed. They had hoped that some cure would restore the man to his family, so he could live a normal life. When I said that his life was remarkable and quite meaningful, they could not understand me. They saw his life as a tragedy, and that is why they were sad. But the great tragedies of Shakespeare are meaningful to many people, so perhaps the meaning depends on how those lives affect us.

I haven't seen that movie, but I'll make it a point to find it. When those people said they were saddened by the ending, but you were not, it fits with what I was saying about how we are psychologically affected by the question of the meaning of life.

312

I see. It does seem hard to talk about the question of whether life has meaning without attaching some notion of duration. Perhaps that is one of the attractions of many religions that hold out the promise of an eternal existence after we die. Recall that Kierkegaard maintained that if death leads to oblivion, then life is empty. That is a powerful psychological lure that attracts believers. But does the answer to whether life has meaning depend solely on a belief in an eternal realm? Can meaning exist in some other way? For instance, gardening gives many people immense pleasure. It is pleasant, forward-looking, and gratifying. When a garden reaches its full-bloom, it provides solace for some, aesthetic appreciation for others, a contemplative space for still others. All those things are saturated with meaning.

But what if the garden fails? Suppose it rains too much or not enough, or blight kills everything. Is it still meaningful?

The failure of the garden to reach its full potential does not nullify the individual experiences of the person involved in caring for it. The daily caring and nurturing are experiences that are meaningful as they occur, and perhaps as later memories. Might there be sadness if things fail? Sure, but the experience of sadness does not dissolve the other experiences.

But suppose we accept that God doesn't exist, and instead we believe, as science tells us, that life arose by chance. Would life still have meaning?

A great question. Since our experiences are real, they can be the source of meaning, regardless of whether life arose by chance. We can find meaning in the sense of wonder we experience as we interact with the world, how excited we are when we discover something new, paint a picture, touch an animal, read a book, watch a movie, listen to music, or have a conversation. So, even if life arose through a series of improbable events, that should inspire us to embrace the idea that our highly improbable life is indeed meaningful.

But the improbability of our existence in an immense universe can also lead us to think that our lives are completely insignificant, because when humans cease to exist, then our acts and lives were mere fleeting instances in the long, long duration of the universe. Whatever we do will come to nothing.

But even if our acts and lives are, as you say, "mere fleeting instances," I do not see why duration should have anything to do with whether or not our acts and lives have meaning. One minute of happiness can sustain a person for a lifetime. For some people that is enough.

Oh my, I just heard the train conductor announce that we are arriving at the station where I must get off. Are you getting out at this stop, too?

No, I am continuing on until the final stop. Even though our conversation will soon end, it will linger in our minds for a while. And even though our memories of it will end someday, the immediate experience of having the conversation, and the later experiences we will have whenever we remember it, provide it with meaning. That it will eventually disappear does not deprive it of being meaningful.

I never expected this train ride would go by so fast, and to open up many things for me to explore further. I hope we can meet again someday.

There is a chance.

References

Chapter 1

Helen Keller, *The Story of My Life*, 1903.

Chapter 4

Cesare Beccaria, *On Crimes and Punishments,* 1764.

Bertrand Russell, *Introduction to Mathematical Philosophy*, 1919.

Chapter 5

The Ring of Gyges. Plato, *Republic,* translated by Benjamin Jowett, 1892.

J. R. R. Tolkien, *Lord of the Rings,* 1954.

Anthony Burgess, *A Clockwork Orange,* 1962.

Stanley Kubrick, *A Clockwork Orange*, Warner Brothers, 1971.

Johann W. von Goethe, *Faust, a Tragedy,* translated by Bayard Taylor, 1870.

Robert Louis Stevenson, *Strange Case of Dr. Jekyll and Mr. Hyde,* 1886.

Oscar Wilde, *The Picture of Dorian Gray,* 1890.

Chapter 9

Robert Nozick, "Fiction," *Ploughshares,* vol. 6, no. 3, 1980.

Chapter 12

Blaise Pascal, *The Thoughts of Blaise Pascal*, translated by Charles Kegan Paul, 1901.

Chapter 13

Probability Theories. Here is a good start. https://plato.stanford.edu/entries/probability-interpret/

Mondegreen. Maria Konnikova, "Excuse Me While I Kiss This Guy," *The New Yorker*, December 10, 2014.

Martingale System. There are many places on the Internet where you can find more information.

The Three Door problem has also been called the "Monty Hall problem," associated with the game show "Let's Make a Deal." You can look for further discussion here:

https://math.ucsd.edu/~crypto/Monty/montybg.html

Chapter 16

Zeno's paradox. Here is one source: https://plato.stanford.edu/entries/paradox-zeno/

Chapter 17

Heinrich Heine, *On the History of Religion and Philosophy in Germany*, 1834 (the quote from Hegel may perhaps be apocryphal).

Georg W. F. Hegel, *The Philosophy of History*, translated by J. Sibree, Batoche Books, 2001.

Martin Heidegger, *Being and Time*, translated by John Macquarrie and Edward Robinson, Harper, 2008.

Immanuel Kant, *Critique of Pure Reason,* translated by J. M. D. Meiklejohn, 1900.

Chapter 18
Bertrand Russell, *A History of Western Philosophy,* 1945.
Bertrand Russell, *The Philosophy of Logical Atomism,* 1918.
René Descartes, *Discourse on Method,* translated by John Veitch, 1880.

Chapter 19
Plato, *Meno,* translated by Benjamin Jowett, 1892.
Plato, *Republic,* translated by Benjamin Jowett, 1892.

Chapter 20
Raymond Smullyan, *What Is the Name of This Book?*, Dover Publications, 2011.
Raymond Smullyan, *This Book Needs No Title*, Touchstone, 1986.
Nicholas W. Best, "Lavoisier's Reflections on Phlogiston," *Foundations of Chemistry,* 17 (2). 2015.

Chapter 21
René Descartes, *Meditations on First Philosophy,* translated by John Veitch, 1901.
William James, "Does Consciousness Exist?" *Journal of Philosophy, Psychology and Scientific Methods*, 1904.

Thomas Nagel, "What is it Like to Be a Bat?" *The Philosophical Review*, LXXXIII, 4, 1974.

Patricia Smith Churchland, "The Hornswoggle Problem," *Journal of Consciousness Studies*, 3, 1996.

John Locke, *An Essay Concerning Human Understanding,* 1690.

Paul-Henri d'Holbach, *The System of Nature,* translated by H. D. Robinson, 1868.

Baruch Spinoza, *Ethics,* translated by R.H.M. Elwes, 1883.David Hume, *A Treatise of Human Nature,* 1777.

David Hume, *An Enquiry Concerning the Principles of Morals,* 1777.

Friedrich Nietzsche, *Beyond Good and Evil,* translated by Helen Zimmern, 1913.

Chapter 22

Thomas Hobbes, *Leviathan,* 1651.

John Stuart Mill, *Liberty,* 1859.

Chapter 23

Plato, *Apology,* translated by Benjamin Jowett, 1891.

Chapter 24

Søren Kierkegaard, *Fear and Trembling,* translated by Walter Lowrie, Princeton University Press, 1941.